"Many of us have heard the term 'marketplace ministry' but we do not understand its true meaning or the most effective approach in growing God's kingdom within the stream of commerce. This book is a must-read for individuals interested in learning about marketplace ministry. It is the story of God's faithfulness to one of God's faithful servants, Buddy Childress, who established a national model for marketplace ministry in the capital region of Virginia. His story will benefit those interested in learning the biblical principles to follow in order to establish a successful ministry that fulfills the Great Commission."

—BARRY E. DUVAL
  President & CEO, Virginia Chamber of Commerce

"Whether you minister to the marketplace or simply work in it, you will be inspired by Buddy Childress' forty-year journey with Needle's Eye Ministries, so lovingly articulated in this delightful book."

—THOMAS E. GOTTWALD
  Chairman, President, and CEO, NewMarket Corporation

"Few people have done more to bring the gospel to bear on the marketplace than my friend, Buddy Childress. As the founder of Needle's Eye Ministries, a thriving marketplace ministry in Richmond, Virginia, Buddy has blazed a trail for forty years. I have preached that 'your job is your pulpit' and 'your colleagues are your congregation,' but Buddy has put it into practice. In Navigating the Needle's Eye, Buddy unpacks the lessons he's learned and provides a map for those called into the marketplace. This book will both challenge and encourage!"

—MARK BATTERSON
  Lead Pastor, National Community Church, Washington D.C.

"In an age when style often out-points substance and social media outlets afford everyone their fifteen minutes of fame, it's nice to know that there are some people who shun the limelight and 'just do it!' Such is the case of Buddy Childress, Founder and Executive Director of Needle's Eye Ministries in Richmond, Virginia. For over 40 years he has faithfully served the local business community without the fuss and fanfare that so often accompany successful ventures, but now he tells his fascinating story with a refreshing blend of grace and alacrity, and it's a story that needs to be told. Graduating from Gordon-Conwell Theological Seminary in 1977, no doubt with a choice of ministries available to him, he had decided already to take a 'road less traveled' and dedicated his entire life to the fledgling and uncertain world of marketplace ministry. Modern denizens of the faith at work movement will no doubt recognize some of the programs and events that he employed in his mission to the business community, not even realizing that he was a genuine pioneer in their field. But pastors and Christians of all stripes will be inspired by his unrelenting faith in the Word of God, his devotion to prayer, and his willingness to make difficult choices, trusting that God would provide for all of his needs. That said, this isn't so much a book about a man's faith in God, it's more about God's faith in a man, to do as he was directed and to give all the glory back to him. Richmond has been blessed by this ministry and readers will be equally blessed in the telling of the story."

—KENNETH J. BARNES
FRSA, Mockler-Phillips Chair in Workplace Theology and Business Ethics, Gordon-Conwell Theological Seminary

"In *Navigating the Needle's Eye*, Buddy Childress has written a powerful and inspirational book that lays out both the spiritual underpinnings and practical truths that led to 40 years of ministry in Richmond, Virginia, in what some have called a one-of-a-kind Christian marketplace ministry. The Great Commission, Childress writes, is God's command that 'we are all called by Christ' to live and spread His word, and that businessmen and women have both the opportunity and responsibility to be His disciples; that their impact from Monday through Friday can be greater than that of a vocational minister or priest on Sunday. At times autobiographical and nostalgic, the book traces Childress' life-changing conversion in 1973, to his rich experience in seminary which led to four decades of leading a robust, Christ-centered marketplace ministry called Needle's Eye."

—RICHARD CULLEN
    Partner and former Chairman, McGuireWoods
    Former Attorney General, Commonwealth of Virginia

"Needle's Eye has been a tremendous blessing in my life and in so many others' lives. In less than one month, I met with three influential business leaders, who shared their testimony with me, all three of whom came to know Christ through Needle's Eye. That made me want to get involved with Needle's Eye, and I'm so glad that I did. Through my small group of Christian marketplace leaders and Buddy's guidance, I view my workplace so much differently now. I view it as a ministry—one in which I can be a witness to people who will never attend church and who have their "BS radar" up regarding Christians and whether they're really any different. So many times, I'm doing so out of my weaknesses, but I have a new found joy and sense of fulfillment for my work as I approach it as doing God's work there. Navigating the Needle's Eye is a must-read for anyone who wants to be a witness in their workplace and to find a higher calling for their work."

—SHAWN BOYER
    Founder of Snagajob, Owner and Founder of goHappy

Navigating the Needle's Eye

Navigating the Needle's Eye

Forty Years of Ministry to
Business and Professional People

Judson E. Childress Jr.

Foreword by Robert E. Cooley

RESOURCE *Publications* · Eugene, Oregon

NAVIGATING THE NEEDLE'S EYE
Forty Years of Ministry to Business and Professional People

Resource Publications
An Imprint of Wipf and Stock Publishers
199 W. 8th Ave., Suite 3
Eugene, OR 97401

www.wipfandstock.com

PAPERBACK ISBN: 978-1-5326-8507-1
HARDCOVER ISBN: 978-1-5326-8508-8
EBOOK ISBN: 978-1-5326-8508-8

Manufactured in the U.S.A.   JULY 9, 2019

To Laura, my wife of fifty years, whose love, forgiveness, perseverance, and grace have enabled me to minister to rich young rulers, rather than become one.

Contents

Foreword

WHAT BUSINESSMAN-TURNED-MARKETPLACE MINISTER BUDDY Childress has proclaimed and practiced for the past forty years is finally in print. His passion, which has influenced thousands of business persons and professionals, has been set down in this book.

Buddy is forthright and clear about his passion—that all believers in Christ are called to ministry. This passion has been forged in the context of marketplace ministry, and this book tells the story of personal calling, spiritual disciplines, and the foundational truths of Needle's Eye Ministries. Prayer, trust, obedience, and listening to the Spirit are set forth as essentials for effective ministry. It is clear that biblical reflection done in the context of ministry sharpens an understanding of the Bible and empowers further ministry to the glory of God.

Chapters 7 and 8 are a how-to manual for effective marketplace ministry. Chapter 9 provides keys to staying relevant. New twists are provided. The book ends with an effort to discern the future of Needle's Eye Ministries in a changing world. As a result, a freshly-minted statement of vision will guide the ministry—"To see Metro Richmond prosper and rejoice through the transformed lives of men and women passionately pursuing Jesus Christ in their workplaces." This vision gives direction to hopes, desires, imaginations, and courage.

This book provides the encouragement that is necessary to persevere to meaningful and relevant marketplace ministry. It provides an overall picture of marketplace ministry that is full of excitement, and is grounded in forty years of experience and success. It has a powerful message! Today is an historical moment of opportunity for communities of faith to make a commitment to encourage business people and professionals, through God's grace, to come into a transforming personal relationship with the Living Christ.

ROBERT E. COOLEY
President Emeritus, Gordon-Conwell Theological Seminary

Preface

THIS BOOK ACTUALLY BEGAN years ago as a labor of love. Four people who love Jesus Christ, have hearts for the lost, get it when it comes to equipping the saints for the work of ministry, and care deeply about yours truly (and vice versa) encouraged me to write this book.

Pete Hammond, former Vice President and Director of Inter-Varsity's Marketplace Ministry, and my wife, Laura, were the first ones. When Pete would come through Richmond, he would often stay with us. In the several years prior to his unexpected death, those visits usually included Pete and Laura teaming up to strongly encourage me to write a book about Needle's Eye.

A few years later, John Hershman, former senior pastor of West End Assembly of God, got on the bandwagon. John and I were at Gordon-Conwell together and started in ministry in Richmond at the same time.

Finally, there was Dr. Robert E. Cooley, President Emeritus of Gordon-Conwell Theological Seminary. Over the past five years, Bob has been encouraging, insightful, available, and a bit tenacious about this book. My thanks and appreciation to all of these highly treasured supporters.

Beyond those who encouraged me to write this book, there are countless others I would like to thank, others whom God has used in wonderful ways to impact the outreach efforts of Needle's Eye. From members of our Board of Directors, our other boards and councils, to our team over the years, luncheon speakers, small group leaders, Needles Eye 911 volunteers, Career Transition Ministry leaders, Second Half leadership, monthly luncheon meal teams, and many others, God has blessed us with innumerable marketplace people who have delivered marketplace ministry.

This book seeks to combine the how-to(s) of marketplace ministry with the biblical principles that should undergird any ministry. While highlighting some of its historic beginnings, I have tried to make this book relevant for today's marketplace ministry. I would suggest its foundational truths are for all believers of any day.

I think that any book which attempts to cover forty years has the potential for challenges with facts and details. Consequently, I have researched our corporate files, archives, and read through numerous Needle's Eye board meeting minutes. I am confident that the vast majority of the specifics, and the dating of events, are accurate.

I have not been able to include all of the ministries and outreaches that we have implemented over the years. What you will see are most of the primary ones, which also depict our "Twelve Truths over 40 Years" (see Addendum).

A number of friends and colleagues have helped to make this book possible. I would like to thank Andrew Fuller, President of World Horizons, for his time and effort in compiling from his diary a two-page memo on the prayer movement in Richmond in the 1990s. To Doctors Bob Andrews and Chuck Smith of Virginia Commonwealth University, and Tony Wilson, former Business Development Manager for Averett University, my gratitude for their thoughts, memories, and leadership of the Friday morning Bible study.

I am indebted to Shawn Boyer, founder of Snagajob and goHappy; Ken Banks, President and CEO of IPC Technologies; and Col. Doug Middleton, former Chief of Police of Henrico County, for their time and insights relative to technology and the future.

Finally, I would like to thank my eleventh-hour editor, Weldon Bradshaw, and my final and tenacious proofreader, my wife Laura.

What you are about to read is the story of a powerful, faithful, and loving God using changed, yet imperfect people to impact a community for his purposes and glory. Thank you, Lord Jesus, for the privilege of being a part of this story for over forty years!

BUDDY CHILDRESS
Richmond, Virginia
July, 2018

CHAPTER ONE

How Needle's Eye Ministries Came to be

WHEN I WAS A young businessman, I got things done. I regularly met my quotas, and I made good money for someone my age. Toward the end of my business career I increasingly became frustrated and felt unfilled. Success had become routine, and the results were hollow. I am so thankful that God reached out and turned me in the right direction!

Let me give you some background. My dad was one of ten children. He grew up in the Great Depression, and his family was so poor that several of the children were sent to live in an orphanage until the family could afford to feed them. My father was one of them. Those hard times made an indelible impression on him, and perhaps not surprisingly, he vowed his life would be different. He would never allow himself to be poor.

In his mid-twenties my dad started his own stationery and printing company. A minimum ten-hour workday and a sixty-hour workweek became the norm. His life was an American story of someone committed to pulling himself up by his bootstraps. His work ethic affected me even as a young boy. During the summers, beginning at age ten, he would have me sweep floors or clean bathrooms at his place of business. As a result of those long hours and hard work, my father was fairly successful and deserves credit for having been a good provider. In spite of his success, however, he was always looking over his own shoulder.

In somewhat of a skewed way, the song, "Cats in the Cradle" reflects some of what my life became. The son of the man, singing that he was going to be like his dad, that could have been me. Although I didn't want to become like my father, his work style and mentality became my own, and they led to priorities and values that were way out of order. What kind of car I drove, the people I knew, where we lived, and how much money I made topped my list. These goals can give impetus to achieving the American dream. However, it is important to keep things in perspective and to recognize that position, wealth, and prestige are not what's most important in the long run. I was blind to that. My priorities were out of order, and that led to poor decision-making.

Let me share one example: I was a good basketball player in high school, and when the time came for college, I accepted the promise of a partial scholarship to play for a Division II team. To get the scholarship, though, I had to make the team, and the team I had to make had been to the NCAA Division II Tournament the prior year—with no seniors. Because I had been very successful in my high school playing career, it did not occur to me that I might not succeed. I had been an honor graduate in high school, so I assumed I could get away with just studying the night before a test or exam. Plus, socializing and fraternity parties and having a good time were a lot of fun!

The coach called me into his office after about thirty days. "Buddy, you are going to have to make a decision," he said. "You're going to have to decide if you want to play basketball or be in a fraternity, because it doesn't appear you can do both." Late nights and partying were not helping my playing ability. He saw that, but I didn't. Three weeks later, he called me into his office again. "Remember the conversation we had before?"

"Yes, sir."

"Well, this is the second and the last one. You are no longer on the team." That may have been the biggest disappointment of my life up to that point, and there was no one to blame but myself. However, as they say, life goes on.

During my sophomore year, I began dating Laura, the woman who is now my wife. We became engaged the next fall and were married at the end of my junior year. That is likely the reason I was able to finish college on time, and graduate with a "Gentleman's C." Being married caused me to grow up a little!

So there I was, married and a college grad. It was an intense time during the Vietnam War era, but thankfully, I was able to get into the National Guard. After serving full time for five months, I came home, and a month or so later, I took a sales job with Xerox.

It was 1970, and Xerox was the only copier company with a machine that had the capability of putting an image on plain paper. That meant practically no competition, which made it a great place to be for a hard-charger like me. What was most important in my life had to do with my job, even though I was married and now the father of a young child. I was with Xerox almost three years and was promoted three times.

Looking back, it's clear I was neither an attentive or sensitive husband nor an engaged father. Success, how much money I made, my job title, my responsibilities, and the house and neighborhood in which we lived were what was important. I was in my element! My territory, which included Charlottesville, Virginia and the surrounding area, accounted for annual revenue of almost $1.5 million—about ten million in today's dollars.

That period of my life ended when my father had a heart attack and we returned to Richmond so I could help run his company until he recovered. I knew that when he did come back to work, I'd move on because we did not work well together. There was a lot of hurt, and there were emotional scars from my relationship with my father. For example, even though I'd excelled in basketball and started for three years, I was able to count on one or two hands the number of times he had come to one of my games. Conversely, my mother and I were very close. She came to all of my games, but died unexpectedly the summer before my junior year in college.

Time went by, and my father returned to work. I left and went to work for New England Mutual. I sold life insurance and mutual funds, and I did quite a bit of estate planning for physicians and attorneys. However, before long something happened which I would not have been able to imagine a few years earlier. It came about because of a promise I'd made to my wife.

I had promised her that when our son was two, we'd go back to church together. For me, since we already went on Christmas Eve and Easter, I saw no reason to overdo it. But this was not about me; rather it was about my wife and our son. Growing up, my family had gone to church from time to time, but it had no impact on me. I had actually attended and successfully completed a Communicants' Class and become a member of the church. Looking back, I realize now that I was not a believer. I didn't know what it meant to be a true Christian.

Honoring my promise to Laura, we started going to the church where she grew up and we had been married. There was a new associate pastor who had just graduated from seminary. He'd grown up in Wisconsin and was a Packers fan and, next to the Washington Redskins, it didn't get any better than the Packers. He was intelligent and a sharp dresser. So for all the wrong reasons, I decided to listen when he stepped into the pulpit.

That morning I heard a message I had not heard before, which now seems hard to believe. If I had heard it, it certainly hadn't registered. The message was about a personal God who knew me to my core and loved me in spite of who I was and what I had become. I sat in the pew thinking, "If this is true, if there is really a God who knows me, really knows me, there's no way he could possibly love me." I knew myself! To some extent my wife knew me, but she didn't know me as well as I did. The idea of being forgiven just did not seem possible, not with the long list of sins I carried around.

At that moment, God was convicting me, and it was so unsettling! When the sermon ended and the final hymn began, I took Laura by the hand, went out into the aisle, and headed straight out of the sanctuary, wanting nothing more than to get out of that church.

God had something else in mind. The preacher had already left the pulpit and was standing by the door. I was trapped! The pastor stopped us, introduced himself and said he was glad I had come. He said he was teaching a Sunday school class for young married couples and he would like Laura and me to come. "No way," I thought. "Once I get out of here, you won't see me again." Then he added that the class was studying controversial issues in the Bible. That was intriguing to me. I was interested and immediately thought, "What a field day I could have with this!"

Again, God had other plans. Something happened inside me over the next few days. Saturday evening came, and I found myself asking Laura if she wanted to go to church, *and* Sunday school. She, of course, said, "Yes." When we arrived, we learned that the topic of the morning was the resurrection. I was pretty sure God existed, but I had always had a problem with the resurrection. It simply did not compute. I could not process how it was possible, and if I could not process it, as far as I was concerned, it could not have happened.

About ten minutes into the lecture, I raised my hand. The pastor, whose name was Jeff, called on me. He remembered my name, and that impressed me.

Even so, I said, "Jeff, I appreciate what you are saying, but I don't believe all this crap." Laura was next to me, and I knew she was wishing a trap door would open underneath her so she could gently escape to the room below. Definitely not Laura's favorite memory!

"Oh, okay," he said. He pointed to a stack of books on the table, not one of which had been written by a theologian or pastor. They all were by professors and researchers from academia, heads of departments of archaeology and experts in other disciplines, individuals with solid credentials anyone would buy. That was a good thing, because I would have had a problem otherwise. I wanted an objective opinion.

Jeff took a piece of chalk and using these sources listed all the theories of what happened two thousand years ago. Then he eliminated them one by one—the twin brother theory, the swoon theory, and so forth—until only one was left. I had just been led down a hallway with all the escape doors closing behind me. There was no option but to accept the resurrection as fact.

Our relationship began that day. Jeff took me under his wing. He answered every question I had, stupid or otherwise, at least twice, and was always available to me. He'd come to our house to watch a Packers game. I'd drink the better part of a six-pack, and he'd drink a Coke, but he never criticized me.

Four or five months went by. One evening Jeff and his wife came for dinner. Afterward, we went into the living room for coffee and dessert, and Jeff said, "Buddy, may I ask you some questions?"

"Sure."

"I think you have asked me every question you have about Jesus and who he was, haven't you?"

"Yes, I guess so."

"I've answered them all, right?"

"Yes, you have."

"I think you find yourself at a place where a lot of people find themselves at your stage of spiritual inquiry. You have a lot of knowledge. You understand who Christ is. You understand what he did on the cross, and what he can do for you. Is that right?"

"Yes."

"May I ask you one more question?

"Sure."

"What are you going to do with him?"

I gave him a puzzled look.

"You don't know what I'm talking about, do you?"

I shook my head.

"You need to have an eighteen-inch experience. You need to move that knowledge and understanding from here, to here." (He pointed to his head and then to his heart.) "You may know correct information, but knowing the facts is not enough. It's all about knowing him."

"But how's that done?"

"It's not difficult. A simple and sincere prayer is all that's required. You need to admit you are a sinner, ask for his forgiveness, ask Jesus to come into your life and to change your life, and commit yourself to him. It comes down to permitting Jesus to be Lord of your life."

"Okay, how do I do that?"

"There are a couple of ways. I would be happy to help you pray a prayer like that, or I can give you a piece of literature that explains what we just discussed and has a prayer at the end."

"I'll take the literature!"

Jeff handed me a pamphlet called *The Four Spiritual Laws*, which had been published by what was then called Campus Crusade for Christ and is now known as Cru. Jeff and his wife left our house, Laura went to bed, and I stayed up. I went to the living room and watched the Johnny Carson monologue. I wanted to be certain I was alone and wouldn't be disturbed. Then I read the booklet and said the prayer . . . two times, just to be sure! I figured my list of sins was such that one reading and prayer wouldn't be enough.

That night, in the fall of 1973, my life began to change. Christ became real to me—my personal Lord and Savior. Most people who come to faith do not have a supernatural experience, but I did. A presence engulfed me, as though a vat of warm honey had been poured over me.

I knew my life would change. I wanted it to change, definitely needed it to change! I'd been a successful businessman, but I had not been the sort of businessman I like to encourage people to be today. Certainly I had not been a good husband or father.

Some things changed immediately, certain aspects of my behavior and the language I used. I became interested in and took part in Bible studies and prayer and praise groups. Other changes took longer.

I was now with a good company that offered a product people needed, and I began to see what I was doing as caring for others. Anyone who has been in insurance and has handed a recent widow with two young children a significant check—all she will have to live on for the next few years of her life—understands the importance of that product. Even so, although I continued to do well in business, after about a year I lost my passion for my work. This was scary as this kind of thing had never happened before.

To help me work through this unusual time, I gathered a support group. It included my pastor, as well as a businessman and two other pastors I had come to know. After a few months, each of them said to me he thought God was calling me to leave the business world and to go to seminary. I resisted the thought of that. After several months of prayer, discussion, and contemplation, one asked me if I wanted God to drive the car of my life. I said, "Yes," to which he responded, "Then you have to start the car, get from behind the wheel, let Christ drive it, and see where he takes it."

I had no knowledge of this academic discipline on which to build, so I struggled with the idea for several months. I finally got to the point that I knew it was what God wanted.

Now it was time to share with Laura the direction in which God was leading me. After having two miscarriages since our first son's birth, Laura had just delivered our second son and was still in the hospital. Looking back on the details of my sharing this update, I realize that my timing could have been better.

When Laura was eight months pregnant with our first child, Xerox had moved us from Richmond to Charlottesville. Now we were settled back in Richmond, surrounded by her family's love and support. She had just given birth to our second, long-awaited baby, and I was proposing another move.

In recent years, I had had a couple of other very creative business ventures that had not come to full fruition. Laura reminded me of these and my pattern of diving into whatever I do 500 percent or not at all. She said she was willing to move forward with exploring this step by step. She told me that if the Lord showed us that this move was his will for our lives, she was on board. However, if this was only another of my creative adventures, that was another thing. I already had a job in which God was using me well in the lives of my colleagues and clients.

Jeff, a graduate of Princeton Theological Seminary, told me if he had it to do over he would have gone to Gordon-Conwell Theological Seminary in South Hamilton, Massachusetts. I'd heard of Princeton, but I had never heard of Gordon-Conwell. One of the other pastors recommended it as well, so I applied to Gordon-Conwell.

The question became: Would I be accepted? As I wrote earlier, I had a Gentleman's C average in college. I also had a dubious reputation with the college's administration, having been president of my fraternity the year we went on probation. This appeared likely to be an issue, considering that in addition to a spiritual reference, two references from my college were required. I did not think my advisor, who was in the political science department, would be a problem. However, I was very concerned about getting a reference from someone in the administration. The dean of students was the same person who'd held that position when I was a student there. I called and asked him to go to lunch, and he reluctantly agreed.

When we met together, I told him the whole story. I'm not sure if he was awed by God's power and grace or stunned and in sheer disbelief. He sat stone-faced, not saying a word.

It was now June 1975, and I was sending my application in forty-five days after the deadline had passed. I was truly amazed to be accepted in only eight days! This seemed to confirm we were on the right track and were pursuing what God had in mind.

A second blessing and example of God's grace came when we listed our house for sale, and we sold it for the full asking price after just three days. That gave us the money we needed to live on for the next few years. During this process there were many other answered prayers and indications of God's leading. Next, we took a trip to Massachusetts and found a 1720s large farmhouse that the seminary owned and rented as a duplex to two couples. Our side had three bedrooms, and the heat was included! Plus, it was in a great school district, another priority on our prayer list.

After this house-hunting trip and selling our house in Richmond, I left almost immediately for Massachusetts, as fall classes were starting. Laura began to pack all our belongings, and I returned a few weeks later to load a U-Haul truck. Laura and I, along with Cam (four and a half), Cabell (three months), and our dog, Pilsner, headed to Massachusetts.

Gordon-Conwell turned out to be a wonderful choice. The academics were outstanding, and virtually every professor had an open-door policy. As time went by, many of those professors became much more than academicians to me. They were brothers in Christ and spiritual mentors.

It was at the beginning of my second semester when God made it clear why we were there and what we were going to do. Almost everyone goes to seminary to become a pastor, but in my daily quiet time in the early months of 1976, I began to sense that God was leading and preparing me to begin a ministry to business and professional people back home in Richmond. I had never heard of such a ministry, but over the next two weeks that thought came to me nearly every day during my quiet time. I could not shake it. Finally, I came home one evening and told Laura I thought I knew what we were going to do after seminary.

"What?" she asked.

"I think God's calling us to go home and minister to business and professional people."

Laura said, "You may not believe this, but for the past week or so, that's also what I've been hearing." This was a confirmation of what Laura's thoughts had been all along. She had never seen my gifts as those of a pastor and couldn't imagine God not using my years in business for his purposes in some kind of ministry.

The next morning I went to see my advisor, Dr. J. Christy Wilson, and told him what Laura and I thought the Lord was saying to us.

"What do you think?" I said.

"Well, Buddy, wouldn't it be just like God to use your past for his future?"

We never looked back from that point forward.

Dr. Wilson did more than confirm the wisdom of our decision. He helped me get a course approved by the Academic Affairs Committee—on the second try, I might add. It was called, "Effective Evangelism With Business and Professional People." At that time no books existed for a ministry of that kind, and this was to be a graduate-level course. As a result, I had to do a good deal of parallel theological reading, strategic planning, interviewing, and pragmatic application. In effect, this course laid the foundation for what was to become Needle's Eye Ministries.

I completed the course during that next summer while at home in Richmond. I had accepted a position as a summer youth pastor in order to enable us to come home for the summer and allow me to complete the course while in Richmond. It was during that time that I established our initial Board of Directors. This board consisted of the pastor of the church where I was serving, Jeff, who'd led me to Christ, a businessman, and one of the other pastors who had walked me through the process leading to my seminary decision. When I returned to seminary that fall, I had already switched programs from the pastoral track (MDiv) to a Master of Theological Studies degree. This degree carried a higher academic requirement, but was a year shorter. It provided tremendous flexibility, allowing me to take the courses I needed. Because it enabled us to finish a year sooner, it was another answer to a prayer as our money would be running out at the end of that academic year.

During my final year, the two pastors on my board organized a meeting of Richmond business people to introduce them to this impending ministry. In March, I flew home to attend that meeting. This gathering produced excitement for Needle's Eye and just under three thousand dollars in seed money, gifted from two churches and the eight to ten people present. That would equal about twelve thousand dollars in today's world.

In May 1977, I graduated from seminary, and we moved back to Richmond in June. On July 1, 1977, Needle's Eye Ministries began.

For several years it was a struggle financially, but I can testify that God has always been faithful! Early on I met Sam Jackson, a wonderful Christian businessman who generously rented us our first office for only twenty dollars a month. It was in the basement of an apartment building. As our monetary needs have grown over the years, gifts have always increased, although rarely by more than we needed. That seems to be how God works. He promises to meet our needs, and sometimes provides for our wants as well.

As I mentioned, the independent reading course served to establish a plan for the ministry. Much of it had to do with going

places where businessmen and women could be found, such as
Rotary luncheons and other business club meetings. I also was
able to get a Chamber of Commerce Directory that listed the top
executive of each member business in the Metropolitan Richmond
Region. I began cold calling on them. Sometimes I would send
a letter introducing myself to pave the way. At other times, one
of my board members would do so. We also started having mid-
day, midweek services. Eventually, these became luncheon meetings where we featured local business and professional men and
women as speakers. They shared their stories of faith, how they
met Christ, and how that relationship impacted their work. God
used this format immensely, and Needle's Eye grew.

You may be wondering about the name, Needle's Eye. It came
to me soon after God made it clear what we would be doing. You
are probably familiar with the story of the rich young ruler who
came to Jesus to ask what he needed to do to gain eternal life. Here
is the account from Matthew 19:16–26, (NIV):

> Now a man came up to Jesus and asked, "Teacher, what
> good thing must I do to get eternal life?"
>
> "Why do you ask me about what is good?" Jesus
> replied. "There is only One who is good. If you want to
> enter life, obey the commandments."
>
> "Which ones?" the man inquired.
>
> Jesus replied, "'Do not murder, do not commit adul-
> tery, do not steal, do not give false testimony, honor your
> father and mother,' and 'love your neighbor as yourself.'"
>
> "All these I have kept," the young man said. "What
> do I still lack?"
>
> Jesus answered, "If you want to be perfect, go, sell
> your possessions and give to the poor, and you will have
> treasure in heaven. Then come, follow me."
>
> When the young man heard this, he went away sad,
> because he had great wealth.
>
> Then Jesus said to his disciples, "I tell you the truth,
> it is hard for a rich man to enter the kingdom of heaven.
>
> Again I tell you, it is easier for a camel to go through
> the eye of a needle than for a rich man to enter the king-
> dom of God."

When the disciples heard this, they were greatly astonished and asked, "Who then can be saved?"

Jesus looked at them and said, "With man this is impossible, but with God all things are possible."

As you know, the first commandment is, "You shall have no other gods before me" (Exod 20:3 NIV). The young man's problem was that he had placed his money and possessions ahead of God. Wealth was the most important thing in his life, his number one god. The text says the young man went away "sad." The Greek word used for sad is *lupayo* and means "knowingly sad." He understood what Jesus was telling him, yet he went away anyway. Then Jesus said, "It is easier for a camel to go through the eye of a needle than for a rich man to enter the kingdom of God."

However, Jesus' disciples were astonished! In the minds of first-century Jews, wealth was a sign of God's blessing, and so, in their eyes, God had blessed this young man. Yet Jesus said he would not enter the kingdom of heaven. That seemed to them an incredible contradiction.

So, when the disciples asked, "Who then can be saved?" Jesus said that with man this is impossible, but with God "all things are possible," even getting a camel through the eye of a needle, and even getting a rich man into the kingdom of God.

CHAPTER TWO

A Theology of Work

FROM THE BEGINNING OF Needle's Eye, our target audience has been the business and professional community. Today, as in 1977, the business community affects and shapes our culture more than any other segment of society. Consequently, the kingdom needs to be highly represented in this significant sector of our culture. Additionally, believers need to understand that their secular work is their calling and it is just as important to the kingdom as the work of those who are in vocational ministry and have been to seminary.

Here in the United States we spend 60 percent of our waking hours on the job. That is where the lost are, and that is also where decisions are made that can impact our economy and our communities. The workplace is where millions of peoples' hopes, dreams, and futures are affected. It's also where Christ wants those who are his and a part of that community to find and follow their calling. Our work is important to God because he made us in his image and has commanded us to work ever since the beginning of recorded history. God is a worker and, therefore, we also are to be workers. In this chapter we will look at a biblical theology of work in order to understand how work is viewed and used by God.

In the early 1980s, a group called Marketplace Ministries sponsored a small gathering of like-minded people in Boston.

There were about fifteen of us, including their Executive Director, Dan Smick. All of us were either directing marketplace ministries, working in the business world, or serving as academicians with an interest in the theology of work. One of those present was a young student from Dallas Theological Seminary who presented a draft of his dissertation. This draft became a book which was to become the preeminent work on the theology of work up to that time in the twentieth century. The book was *Your Work Matters to God.* The seminarian was Doug Sherman who, along with Bill Hendricks, shaped and packaged that dissertation not only into a well-read volume, but also into subsequent practical application workbooks and seminars on the workplace, discipleship, and decision-making.

My theology of work had been forming long before I met Doug and Bill, but following that gathering in Boston, the thoughts of those men began to have a significant impact on me in those early years. Before we take a close look at their effects, I think it would be helpful to give some thought to the following questions:

- What were you taught about work when you were growing up?

- What does your job mean to you today?

- What are the good things? What are the negatives? What changes could you make?

- What is the purpose of your job? What should it be?

I believe it is important for each of us to give serious consideration to our work and what it means to us. If you don't enjoy the work you do, perhaps it plays a more significant role in your life than it ought to—as it once did for me. You may be more controlling than you should be because of the emphasis you put on work, which results in a greater need for intricate time management. Your goals for work may not be in line with biblical principles. Work is of primary importance to God and it should be to us. Consequently, it is critical that our faith integrates with and impacts our work. The Bible is clear about this. Look closely at Genesis 1:26–28 (NIV):

> Then God said, "Let us make man in our image, in our likeness, and let them rule over the fish of the sea and the birds of the air, over the livestock, over all the earth, and over all the creatures that move along the ground."
>
> So God created man in his own image, in the image of God he created him; male and female he created them.
>
> God blessed them and said to them, "Be fruitful and increase in number; fill the earth and subdue it. Rule over the fish of the sea and the birds of the air and over every living creature that moves on the ground."

The critical piece of the text above is found in verse 28. It is what theologians call, "The Cultural Mandate." I think of it as God's first work order. As you may know, a work order is what the front office of a business uses to get a job started, explained, delegated to the right department, completed, and shipped. With this work order, God is handing his creation to us and telling us he wants us to do three things:

1. Fill it.
2. Subdue it.
3. Rule over it.

Obviously, in the beginning, the earth needed to be populated. The third point has to do with caring for and having dominion over creation—a topic for another time and setting. It's the second command, to subdue the earth, which I find of particular interest.

According to the Merriam-Webster Dictionary, among the meanings of the word "subdue" are these:

- to conquer and bring into subjection
- to bring (land) under cultivation

This appears to be what God had in mind. God is saying that we have a job to do, he created us for a purpose, and the purpose is to care for the masterpiece he made. The job of the first man, Adam, was to till the garden.

Now have a look at Genesis 2:5 (NIV):

> And no shrub of the field had yet appeared on the earth and no plant of the field had yet sprung up, for the Lord *God had not sent rain on the earth and there was no man to work the ground.* (emphasis mine)

God had not sent rain because no one was there to work the land. A human being was needed first. Scripture is telling us that God intended, from the outset, that we would work. He created us to know and to love him, and he created us to work the garden he put us in. Work is not punishment for man's disobedience, as some may believe. Genesis 2:15 (NIV) says:

> The Lord God took the man and put him in the garden of Eden to work it and take care of it.

Eating the fruit and the subsequent fall did not take place until chapter 3. We can conclude from this that work is good, that work has always been intended, and that God commissioned us to work with him to care for his creation. Work has dramatically changed since the garden. There are now thousands of career options, each possessing the opportunity to affect humankind and shape the culture of workplaces and communities, enabling them to flourish. Work is a godly endeavor. That was how it was in the beginning and how it can be today, provided we adopt the right attitude and do our work with a sense of obedience to God.

Consider a New Testament passage written long after the fall, by the apostle Paul—Romans 8:18–22 (NIV):

> I consider that our present sufferings are not worth comparing with the glory that will be revealed in us. The creation waits in eager expectation for the sons of God to be revealed. For the creation was subjected to frustration, not by its own choice, but by the will of the one who subjected it, in hope that the creation itself will be liberated from its bondage to decay and brought into the glorious freedom of the children of God. We know that

the whole creation has been groaning as in the pains of
childbirth right up to the present time.

The text tells us that creation groans to be made right, as it
was initially. For example, the wind that was initially intended to
cool Adam's brow in the heat of the day now becomes hurricanes
and kills people. Adam's idyllic job of caring for a perfect garden
has become something less desirable. Work has been subjugated
to sin and, therefore, how it is done and the results it produces
are often not godly. (See Gen 3:14–19.) We may see our work as
a way to feather our nest. We may see it as a way to enhance our
image (prestige), or we may see it as drudgery to be endured. None
of that was intended. God wanted our work to be good because
God himself was a worker and "it was very good" (Gen 1:31). He
worked six days to create the earth. He continues to work today in
the lives of those who know him—he works to help them change,
improve, grow, and positively impact all with which they come in
contact: people (including co-workers), places (including workplaces), and things (including creation).

Work is holy. As believers, we need to understand that and
commit to living godly lifestyles Monday through Friday, eight to
five (and, of course, beyond). As beings created in God's image, the
answer is to do what we can to make our work resemble, as closely
as possible, the values, ethics, and love of Christ. The following are
principles we should strive to incorporate in our work:

- We should seek to further God's purposes.
- Our work should give us a sense of purpose.
- We should consider ourselves co-laborers with God.

We can do this by using our work to build relationships and
to care for the people with whom we work, as well as the customers
we serve. As previously stated, we spend 60 percent of our waking hours at work. Work is where we mix with others who may
not know Christ. By showing them how a godly person behaves
and goes about tasks, the status of the work we do is elevated and
incorporates the above principles. When we manifest God's Spirit

in what we do, our work becomes holy, and it follows that, by God's grace, our work becomes our ministry. Because God is a worker and work is God-ordained, the work we do should not be seen as or approached as drudgery. Consider, for example, this passage from Ecclesiastes 5:18–20 (NIV):

> Then I realized that it is good and proper for a man to eat and drink, and to find satisfaction in his toilsome labor under the sun during the few days of life God has given him-for this is his lot. Moreover, when God gives any man wealth and possessions, and enables him to enjoy them, to accept his lot and be happy in his work-this is a gift of God. He seldom reflects on the days of his life, because God keeps him occupied with gladness of heart.

Work and the fruits of our labor are to be enjoyed. This is most likely to happen when we take stock of ourselves, determine what we do well and enjoy, and then use our talents, aptitudes, and abilities to serve others with a sense of joy. In this way we use God's gifts to serve him by serving others, as well as to fulfill our potential. As Paul wrote in Colossians 3:22–24 (NIV):

> Slaves, obey your earthly masters in everything; and do it, not only when their eye is on you and to win their favor, but with sincerity of heart and reverence for the Lord. Whatever you do, work at it with all your heart, as working for the Lord, not for men, since you know that you will receive an inheritance from the Lord as a reward. It is the Lord Christ you are serving.

Paul is not endorsing slavery (see his comments in 1 Tim 1:9, 10; Gal 3:28; Phlm 15, 16). Instead, Paul sees the gospel as a change agent for individuals and society. Realistically, Paul had to work through the existing societal structures, and complicating the matter was the fact that in many of the house churches of this new Christian movement, the membership included both slaves and slave owners, workers and managers, if you will. God cared about how each group lived out their faith because faith in Jesus Christ is what changes individual lives, then relationships, and ultimately the culture. Here is Colossians 4:1:

> Masters, provide your slaves with what is right and fair,
> because you know that you also have a Master in heaven.

In today's world, Paul would have been giving this advice to management—from small retail store managers to Fortune 500 CEOs. Therefore, from the factory floor to the executive suite, Paul's message is that we should work to please God rather than man. In the spirit of loving our neighbors, we should love those we serve as well as those who may serve us. Work is to be done well, and it is to be done in service to the Lord. We cannot go wrong when that is our perspective. Our jobs can become sources of satisfaction—even joy.

Paul also tells us how to go about our work. In 1 Thessalonians 4:11–12 (NIV) he writes:

> Make it your ambition to lead a quiet life, to mind your own business and to work with your hands, just as we told you, so that your daily life may win the respect of outsiders and so that you will not be dependent on anybody.

God, through Paul, is saying to us that winning the respect of others and not being dependent on anyone is important. Later, in 2 Thessalonians 3:10, Paul wrote that work is required of all able-bodied believers. If someone is capable of work, of finding and holding a job, and chooses not to work, that person should not be encouraged to continue that lifestyle. The body of Christ is directed not to support that type of behavior. Paul is saying that someone who claims to be a Christian and does not pull his own weight is a false witness. The same is true of a person who runs a company and makes a lot of money, but does not care for those working for him, or for the community. God wants us to care because he does, and to use the gifts and talents he has given us for his purposes and glory. When Jesus Christ becomes our Lord and Savior, we are no longer ours; we belong to the One who originally gave us life.

In a letter to Titus, one of Paul's mentees, a missionary on the island of Crete, Paul also writes about the ethics and attitudes of work. Here is Titus 2:9–10 (NIV):

> Teach slaves to be subject to their masters in everything, to try to please them, not to talk back to them, and not to steal from them, but to show that they can be fully trusted, so that in every way they will make the teaching about God our Savior attractive.

As was the case with the church in Colossae, it appears that some slaves in Titus' church might have been slaves of owners who were believers. Perhaps these slaves thought their owners ought to treat them better. What Paul is saying is that it is incumbent upon the slaves to have good attitudes and do good work because good behavior and ethics make the gospel attractive.

How does doing good work make the gospel attractive?

The word "attractive," in Greek, is *kosmosin*, the word from which we get "cosmetics." What Paul was saying is that doing good work with good habits, attitudes, and values makes the Christian faith, or the gospel, attractive to those who do not know Christ. The same word is used in Revelation 21:2, when the apostle John described the new heaven and the new earth coming out of the sky. John said, "I saw the Holy City, the new Jerusalem, coming down out of heaven from God, prepared as a bride *beautifully dressed* (emphasis mine) for her husband."

Toward the end of his life, living in exile on the island of Patmos, the apostle John uses the best metaphor he could think of to describe the incredible vision God gives him of the new heaven and earth: "A bride beautifully dressed for her husband" (Rev 21:2). "Beautifully dressed," is also from the Greek word *kosmosin*, the same word Paul used when addressing the impact of work done well in Titus. So it is clear, Paul told Titus, to teach believers to employ good ethics and behavior in their work, because work done well makes the gospel attractive to the world!

If we do our work in a way that sets us apart and wins respect, Paul says we will have a positive effect on our coworkers, clients, and suppliers. The gospel lived out in the world makes its message compelling to the world. I have seen this principle lived out often. For example, a man who was a regular attendee of our lunch meetings years ago had an attractive receptionist/administrative assistant. In the evenings, she was the hostess of an upscale nightclub that had a reputation for being a meeting place for singles. She enjoyed her second job and lived a hard-charging lifestyle. Yet through the care her boss showed her, his other employees, and his clients, she was exposed to the example about which Paul wrote. Her boss also brought her to lunch meetings at Needle's Eye. It took time, but not only did she come to faith, she also became involved with a Christian ministry and ultimately began to lead others to faith.

As I close this chapter on the theology of work, let's go back to that series of four bullet-point questions on page fifteen. How would you now answer them? Do you see a higher purpose in what you do professionally? How might your personality, skill set, and relationships be better used for the purpose of the kingdom? For your co-workers? For your employees?

CHAPTER THREE

The Motivators and Needs of Business and Professional People

IT WASN'T LONG AFTER Needle's Eye began that I started to consider the theology of work in a much more serious and deeper way than I had in the past. It made sense to me to go back in time as far as possible, back to the beginning, to fully understand the nature of man, especially in the context of work. As you know, Adam and Eve had a good life in the first two chapters of Genesis. However, throughout the rest of Genesis and the next sixty-five books of the Bible, we see that the nature and condition of humankind changed from that original, unspoiled time.

Let's take a closer look at chapters 1 and 2 of Genesis. Chapter 1 sets the tone. We see that God was well pleased with everything he made over the first six days. He looked over what he created and proclaimed it very good (1:31). A perfect God created perfection! God created man in his own image:

> So God created man in his own image, in the image of God he created him; male and female he created them. (Gen 1:27 NIV)

There are many implications because of this verse and much can be written about them. Perhaps most important is that in the beginning—having been created in God's image—humans were perfect. They had no sin. They were the crown of creation in that they were the only creatures made in the image of God. Humans are the only ones of God's creation that can reason—the only creatures that have the ability to step outside themselves, metaphorically, to consider and contemplate themselves and God.

Again, Genesis 1:28 states:

> God blessed them and said to them [man and woman], "Be fruitful and increase in number; fill the earth and subdue it. Rule over the fish of the sea and the birds of the air and over every living creature that moves on the ground." (NIV)

The word "rule" (in the Revised Standard Version, "have dominion over") also means "to care for," which indicates we have that responsibility, as well as the duty, to work or subdue the perfect creation God made. So, before the end of the first chapter of the Bible, God has created us, blessed us, and given us the mandate or commission to fill the earth, subdue or work it, and to rule over and care for it.

We see that in the beginning God made man and woman and put them in a perfect and peaceful setting where they were in relationship with God. He also delegated responsibilities to them—in effect making them partners with him. It was a time when there was no sin and, therefore, no feelings of guilt or need for forgiveness.

Let's move to Genesis 2:5 (NIV):

> . . . no shrub of the field had yet appeared on the earth and no plant of the field had yet sprung up, for the Lord God had not sent rain on the earth and there was no man to work the ground . . .

This verse implies that God had always intended to have a partnership with man. That partnership involved God delegating authority to man to carry out what he desired. Consider, for example, Genesis 2:19 (NIV):

> Now the Lord God had formed out of the ground all the beasts of the field and all the birds of the air. He brought

them to the man to see what he would name them; and whatever the man called each living creature, that was its name.

Can you imagine what Adam must have thought when God paraded the beasts and birds before him and told him his job was to name them? To delegate such enormous responsibility validates early on God's commitment to the partnership and his high view of Adam. The idea that he might be incomplete must have been far from Adam's mind.

Genesis continues in 2:20–24 (NIV):

So the man gave names to all the livestock, the birds of the air and all the beasts of the field. But for Adam no suitable helper was found.

So the Lord God caused the man to fall into a deep sleep; and while he was sleeping, he took one of the man's ribs and closed up the place with flesh.

Then the Lord God made a woman from the rib he had taken out of the man, and he brought her to the man.

The man said, "This is now bone of my bones and flesh of my flesh; she shall be called 'woman,' for she was taken out of man."

For this reason a man will leave his father and mother and be united to his wife, and they will become one flesh.

So God created woman out of man because the birds and animals alone were not sufficient. Interestingly, the last verse of chapter 2 goes on to say:

The man and his wife were both naked, and they felt no shame. (Gen 2:25 NIV)

Clearly, humans lived in an idyllic state at this point in the history of the world. Adam and Eve were together and completely exposed—though naked, they felt no shame. Shame and guilt did not exist because sin did not exist. Their surroundings were perfect and peaceful. Adam was to care for creation in a partnership with God, and Adam and Eve were completely accepted for who they were. Why shouldn't they be? After all, Adam and Eve had been made in the image of God.

However, things fell apart in Genesis 3:1–7 (NIV):

> Now the serpent was more crafty than any of the wild animals the Lord God had made. He said to the woman, "Did God really say, 'You must not eat from any tree in the garden?'"
>
> The woman said to the serpent, "We may eat fruit from the trees in the garden,
>
> but God did say, 'You must not eat fruit from the tree that is in the middle of the garden, and you must not touch it, or you will die.'"
>
> "You will not surely die," the serpent said to the woman.
>
> "For God knows that when you eat of it your eyes will be opened, and you will be like God, knowing good and evil."
>
> When the woman saw that the fruit of the tree was good for food and pleasing to the eye, and also desirable for gaining wisdom, she took some and ate it. She also gave some to her husband, who was with her, and he ate it.
>
> Then the eyes of both of them were opened, and they realized they were naked; so they sewed fig leaves together and made coverings for themselves.

The crafty serpent got Eve's attention and provoked her thinking by telling her the reason God did not want her to eat the fruit was that he did not want her to become like him. Obviously, the prospect of becoming like God was a profound temptation. To be like God is to have power—ultimate power. On top of that, prestige comes from being wise, just as it does from being wealthy.

As she considered Satan's temptation, Eve then recognized that the fruit was good for food but also pleasing to the eye. In other words, it not only was nutritious, it was attractive, desirable, because of how it looked. This increased within her a desire to acquire the fruit, just as people today are motivated to acquire wealth and the many attractive possessions money can buy. Often, like Eve, people want things for reasons that go beyond their functional purposes. As Dr. Robert E. Cooley, President Emeritus of Gordon-Conwell Seminary, once said to me in reference to this verse, "The eye gate is critical in the Hebrew in this context. It is a gateway beyond mere observation that leads to desires, to the inner most reality of the heart."

These verses show us the motives that caused Eve to succumb, which, when understood at their core, are basically the desire for power, wealth, and prestige. They not only led Eve to eat the fruit at the beginning of time, they are also the same motivators that today create a large number of problems for business and professional people.

As discussed, Adam and Eve lived in a perfect, idyllic setting before the fall. Until Genesis 3, Adam's and Eve's lives were filled with peace and tranquility. God had given them purpose and his presence in their lives. They were accepted by their loving Father not because of how they had performed, but because of his deep and abiding love for them. Since they were made in God's image, they were perfect and "felt no shame." There was no guilt because there was no sin! Life could not have been better.

Adam and Eve were in the setting and environment that God had intended for them and for us. They were perfectly at peace. They were free from guilt and all its psychological and behavioral ramifications, and they were totally and unconditionally accepted, not because of what they had done, but because of whose they were. These garden conditions are what I call the Spiritual PGA—Peace, relief from Guilt, and Acceptance. Although they helped to define our initial state, they have become, post-fall, our greatest needs. Those first two chapters were in a setting where the Spiritual PGA was in effect and operative. Then along came the temptations presented by the serpent, the first of which was to be like God. The second was wealth in the form of the desire to acquire. The third, gaining wisdom, and therefore prestige, capped it off. Throughout the ages acquiring knowledge and gaining wisdom have been seen as valuable pursuits. Prestige comes from being knowledgeable and wise, just as it does from being wealthy. A person is likely to be extremely well thought of if he or she is seen as wise.

In summary, what we have seen is that we were created and put on earth to have peace, to be without sin, and to be accepted for who we are. However, as a result of what might be called human nature, we opted to move away from the perfect setting and situation. We did so because of an inherent desire for power, wealth, and prestige. Today many of us spend our lives chasing these goals, but in our hearts we need and want to return to that initial state of peace, acceptance, and relief from guilt. We so long for this, but have been corrupted as a result of living in a fallen world, with all its gods and temptations. We have become like dogs chasing our tails, trying to get back where we once were. Often we figuratively (and for some, literally) sell our souls for things we hope will provide the innate peace we once had and, therefore, still seek. We desire and long for the promotion to a corner office with all its status and authority, the second home, the portfolio that promises a secure retirement, and travel at the drop of a hat. We go after power, wealth, and prestige, but what we truly and inherently need is peace, relief from guilt, and acceptance.

Thankfully, there is a peace that passes all understanding. Paul talks about it in Philippians 4:1–7 (NIV):

> Rejoice in the Lord always. I will say it again: Rejoice!
> Let your gentleness be evident to all. The Lord is near.
> Do not be anxious about anything, but in everything, by prayer and petition, with thanksgiving, present your requests to God.
> And the peace of God, which transcends all understanding, will guard your hearts and your minds in Christ Jesus.

What it boils down to is this: when we get to the point that we are willing to allow God into our lives and ask for his direction, he will provide a peace that cannot be purchased and that no material object or other human relationship is able to supply or replace. It is a peace that indeed passes all understanding, the peace we had in Genesis 1 and 2, and it is what we are looking for today.

Unfortunately, many of us attempt to find it in ways that end up creating an even greater lack of it.

In moving from peace to relief from guilt, perhaps one of my favorite personal passages is 1 John 1:8–9 (NIV). John wrote it toward the end of his life to counteract a heresy prevalent around the Mediterranean at the time. The heresy was the belief that if a person was good enough, that person could perhaps reach perfection in this life. Here it is:

> If we claim to be without sin, we deceive ourselves and the truth is not in us.
> If we confess our sins, he is faithful and just and will forgive us our sins and purify us from all unrighteousness.

It seems to me people in our post-modern world do not want to think about guilt. In today's society, everything is based on an individual's perception of things, and different people may see things quite differently. For those who buy into that line of reasoning, there are no absolutes. However, regardless of the mores of our age or one's cultural group, it has been my observation and experience that, deep down, an individual simply does not feel right when he or she has sinned. The difference between right and wrong has been intrinsically written on their hearts (See Romans 2:14–15). Sin makes a person feel uneasy—or, in other words, guilty. So what can be done?

In the passage from 1 John above, we are told that by confessing our sins, God will forgive us and cleanse us of all unrighteousness. In this way, our relationship with God will be put right, we will be freed from guilt, and that is precisely what we want, and need!

What about acceptance? Well, I don't know how much more one can be accepted than to be in a perfect setting, having been delegated the authority to work, govern, and care for what God created. He says, "Here, Adam. Fill it, work it, rule it." That is the first recorded example in history of the management principle of the delegation of authority. This obviously shows that God accepted Adam unconditionally. But what about us today, after the fall? How can we be accepted? Romans 5:8 (NIV) points the way. In it, Paul tells us how God shows his love for us:

> . . . God demonstrates his own love for us in this: While we were *still sinners*, Christ died for us. [emphasis mine]

It's important to let that sink in.

I'd like to think that I would die for someone. For example, if I were in battle, that I'd give my life for a fellow soldier. But the truth is you can never know for sure what you will do until you're in the situation.

I do know one thing. I have four children and ten grandchildren, and I have yet to meet the person for whom I would give up any one of them. Amazingly, God did just that . . . and he did it while we were still sinners! He didn't wait until after we had become good or perfect.

We crave acceptance. We want it not because of our performance, but just because of who we are, warts and all. That's precisely what God offers us because that is precisely what we had and, therefore, what we still need!

The Spiritual PGA—Peace, relief from Guilt, and Acceptance for who we are—is a truth that goes back to the beginning of Scripture. For more than forty years now, those have been principles I have seen God use as I have shared the gospel with others. The seekers I meet typically want peace. Frequently, they have been trying to find it in all the wrong places. They need to be forgiven. They may have done things they do not want to share with anyone, and that's something I personally understand. When it comes to acceptance, everything today seems to be based upon performance, but that is not the case with God! The truth is that it is impossible to be good enough. True acceptance is a gift, just like salvation.

In conclusion, Adam and Eve fell from grace because of their desire to be like God, because of their desire to acquire, and because of their desire to gain prestige. Acting upon those desires took them away from life in a perfect, idyllic, and peaceful setting where they were accepted just for whom they were. That is the pure and faultless place to which we long to return, and the

Spiritual PGA can provide the key to unlock the door. If we fully understand and employ its principles in our conversations with seekers, the Holy Spirit will provide the scriptural and experiential tract needed to bring those seekers the second person of the Trinity, the Lord Jesus Christ.

By God's grace I have seen him do it many times!

Chapter Four

We Each are Called

Two chapters ago, we considered what Scripture has to say about work. In this chapter, we will see what it says about calling. This is one of the most critical issues in the church today, and it has been at least since the beginning of the second century.

The church today is organized quite differently than it was at its beginning when the Lord called twelve ordinary men to help him change the world. As humans often do, over the years we developed systems and a structure influenced by human nature which, as we know, is self-oriented more often than not. Os Guinness, in his book *The Call: Finding and Fulfilling the Central Purpose of Your Life* writes about Eusebius, Bishop of Caesarea, and 4th-century church father:

> Eusebius argues that Christ gave "two ways of life" to his church. One is the "perfect life." The other is the "permitted life." The perfect life is spiritual, dedicated to contemplation and reserved for priests, monks, and nuns. The permitted life is secular, dedicated to action and open to such tasks as soldiering, governing, farming, trading, and raising families, whereas those following the perfect life appear to die to the life of mortals and bear with them nothing earthly but their body, and in mind and spirit to have passed to heaven. Those following the

more humble, more human permitted life have a kind of secondary piety.[1]

The division of the kingdom into two classes has become known as the "sacred-secular divide." This has been around since before the 4th century and, to some degree, we still struggle with it in the church today. We do so because in many ways we have professionalized the ministry. For centuries, the church has put all the work of the kingdom in the laps of professionals. Pastors and pastoral counselors preach, lead small groups, and do just about everything else. A friend, colleague, and mentor of mine, Pete Hammond, had something to say about this. Pete was the founder of InterVarsity's Marketplace Subdivision, a vice president of InterVarsity, and a board member of *Christianity Today*. He said, "Because of this sacred-secular divide, the rest of the kingdom (the "permitted life believers") was relegated to praying, paying, and obeying."

That may be a strong statement, but in many ways it was, and remains true to a good degree.

In Ephesians 4:11–12 (NIV), the apostle Paul writes:

> It was he who gave some to be apostles, some to be prophets, some to be evangelists, and some to be pastors and teachers, to prepare God's people for works of service, (to equip the saints for the work of ministry, ESV) so that the body of Christ may be built up.

Paul is saying that all believers are called to do the work of ministry and that pastors are primarily responsible for equipping nonpastors to use their God-given gifts to do the work of ministry. This unequivocally means that we believers are all called to ministry. The principle of calling goes all the way back to the Pentateuch, the first five books of the Old Testament. Perhaps the most obvious example of work and calling is found in Exodus during the time when the Jews were in the wilderness building the tabernacle. Read what the Lord said to Moses about the people who were going to do the work. This is Exodus 31:1–6 (NIV):

1. Os Guinness, *The Call* (Nashville: W Publishing Group, 2003), 32.

> Then the Lord said to Moses, "See, I have chosen Bezalel son of Uri, the son of Hur, of the tribe of Judah, and I have filled him with the Spirit of God, with skill, ability and knowledge in all kinds of crafts to make artistic designs for work in gold, silver and bronze, to cut and set stones, to work in wood, and to engage in all kinds of craftsmanship. Moreover, I have appointed Oholiab son of Ahisamach, of the tribe of Dan, to help him. Also I have given skill to all the craftsmen to make everything I have commanded you."

The word "chosen" in verse 2 ("see, I have *chosen* Bezalel son of Uri") is the same word in the Greek translation of the Jewish Scriptures, the Septuagint, as the word "call" in the New Testament. Therefore, Bezalel was "called" by God. But he wasn't called to be a priest or a Levite. Bezalel and his friend Oholiab were called to be craftsmen. This is the first example in the Bible of God filling someone with his Spirit, and it was not a priest or a prophet. It was a craftsman, a "blue-collar" worker who loved God and had a calling because he was God's.

Each of us is unique with different gifts and skills. These two men who were to be used in the work to construct the tabernacle were normal, everyday people. They were called because they were God's. They had certain skills that he had given them that were to be used to do good work and thereby bring glory and honor to him. Clearly, God chooses ordinary people for his work.

If you look at people in the Bible whom we hold dear, the ones whose stories we tell to our children and grandchildren, you will find the majority were ordinary people. (See Addendum: Calling, a Variety of Experiences.) This includes most of the followers of Jesus. We tell stories about Daniel, who was a consultant to a king, and David, a warrior, king, and man who had many flaws. For all his faults, David was a man after God's own heart. Noah was a shipbuilder and Esther a queen. These biblical heroes were not professional clergy. I have a seminary degree and have been ordained. God called me from business to follow that path, but my story is atypical. Scripturally, it is not the norm.

Work is extremely important to God, so it is important to understand the biblical concept of calling as we move forward to see what God has in mind for the body of Christ and, therefore, for us. When thinking about Bezalel and Oholiab, my mind also goes to Psalm 139:13–16 and Jeremiah 1:5, because together they lay context for the idea of calling. David wrote it hundreds of years before Christ:

> For you created my inmost being;
> you knit me together in my mother's womb.
> I praise you because I am fearfully and wonderfully made;
> your works are wonderful,
> I know that full well.
> My frame was not hidden from you
> when I was made in the secret place,
> when I was woven together in the depths of the earth.
> Your eyes saw my unformed body;
> all the days ordained for me were written in your book
> before one of them came to be.

God created David to be a king. As mentioned, he was a man after God's own heart even though he was flawed and imperfect. David loved God, and he gave David the grid (the unique combination of our gifts, abilities, and interests) to be who he was. My grid is different than David's, although I am also a flawed man. I have certain gifts and abilities, and I have voids in my personality, as we all do. For example, if I were in college trying to obtain a degree in engineering, I'd be in trouble! Actually, I'd still be in undergraduate school! I do not have the gifts and abilities to learn and apply the principles of that discipline.

What Psalm 139, Exodus 31:1–6, and other texts are saying is that we all are called and have different gifts. The Old Testament talks about how God made us and formed us in our mother's womb. It talks about how some of us are craftsmen who are to accomplish certain tasks, such as the building of the tabernacle. We need to understand that every believer who comes to know God in Christ has been called to him and for him. Every believer has a purpose to fulfill and a job (or jobs) to do. They are part of his plan for that individual, and that individual is part of God's plan for the kingdom.

In Jeremiah 1:5 (NIV), God says:

> Before I formed you in the womb I knew you,
> before you were born I set you apart;
> I appointed you as a prophet to the nations.

Before Jeremiah's life began, his life was determined. Although this text specifically refers to Jeremiah, it reveals a God who knew each of us before birth and shaped our lives for his purposes. As believers in Christ, we see God's hand in all our lives through the context of calling.

What about the New Testament? Has the concept of calling been continued or perhaps even expanded? One of the primary words for calling in the New Testament is *klétos*, which appears ten times. Let's begin with Romans 1:1, 6–7 (NIV):

> Paul, a servant of Christ Jesus, called to be an apostle and set apart for the gospel of God . . . And you also are among those who are called to belong to Jesus Christ. To all in Rome who are loved by God and called to be saints: Grace and peace to you from God our Father and from the Lord Jesus Christ.

In the first verse, which is a greeting at the beginning of this letter to the Romans, Paul talks about his function and says he is a servant of Jesus, "called" to be an apostle. Then, in verses 6 and 7 he says, "And you also are among those who are called to belong to Jesus Christ. To all in Rome who are loved by God and called to be saints." You might think that since there is more than one word for "call" in Greek, a different word would be used for one's function/profession, i.e. "called" to be an apostle, as compared to "called" to belong to Jesus Christ or "called" to be saints. However, that is not the case. The same word is used in verse 1 that is used in verses 6 and 7.

Of the ten times *klétos* appears in the New Testament, only twice is it used to represent a function, role, or job (Rom 1:1, and

1 Cor 1:1). The other eight times (Matt 22:14; Rom 1:6–7, 8:28; 1 Cor 1:2, 24; Jude 1; and Rev 17:14) the word "call" is used in the context of those who are "called to be holy," i.e., "called according to his purposes," "we preach Christ crucified, a stumbling block to those whom God has called," and so on. (See addendum.)

In the eight out of ten times the word *klétos* appears in the New Testament, it is used to mean "called to a person," not "called to a function." We are *called* to Christ. He has formed us in our mother's womb and given us the gifts, abilities, and interests (the "grid") we have. Isn't it logical to assume that once we are his we are to use those gifts to do his work right where he has placed us? He made us who we are and gifted us to do and be where we are in order to fulfill his purposes in and through us. Some are called to kingdom work as professionals—evangelists, pastors, and teachers—but we are all called to Christ, and gifted by him to do what we do professionally for him. This elevates work done Monday through Friday in the highways and byways of life to the same level of importance as the work done in pulpits on Sundays. One could even argue that the work done in the world Monday through Friday is even more critical because that is where nonbelievers are. They often are not in church on Sunday, but they have to be at work on Monday!

What are some of the implications of this understanding of calling? Paul writes in Romans 8:18–23 about the effect of the fall, about what happened and still happens (NIV):

> I consider that our present sufferings are not worth comparing with the glory that will be revealed in us. The creation waits in eager expectation for the sons of God to be revealed. For the creation was subjected to frustration, not by its own choice, but by the will of the one who subjected it, in hope that the creation itself will be liberated from its bondage to decay and brought into the glorious freedom of the children of God.
>
> We know that the whole creation has been groaning as in the pains of childbirth right up to the present time. Not only so, but we ourselves, who have the firstfruits

of the Spirit, groan inwardly as we wait eagerly for our
adoption as sons, the redemption of our bodies.

Everything has been affected by the fall. Sin and death per-
meate the culture. Birds die. Floods happen. Tornadoes destroy
homes, crops, and infrastructure that was initially built to make
our lives easier. Everything has been affected. Creation groans to
be put back right, but how can that happen? Ultimately, it will not
happen until Christ returns. In the meantime, those who have
come to know him and are therefore called by him have God-given
responsibilities. They are to use the gifts they have been given and
the work they do to bring the kingdom into the world. They should
not wait for the world to come to the kingdom as it does on Sunday
mornings or Wednesday nights.

Sundays and Wednesday nights are important, but those
times and places are for believers. Nonbelievers aren't likely to be
in church at those times. However, they will be at work, eight to
five, Monday through Friday (or variations thereof). This is where
the majority of our waking hours are spent. Work is where we can
reclaim the culture and creation. We can do it by using the gifts we
have been given. It is our obligation to do so because we have been
called to him and, therefore, to his purposes.

Let's look at the Great Commission. I refer to this, tongue-in-
cheek, as God's second work order. Not long before the ascension,
Jesus said to the disciples in Matthew 28:19–20 (NIV):

> Therefore go and make disciples of all nations, baptizing
> them in the name of the Father and of the Son and of the
> Holy Spirit, and teaching them to obey everything I have
> commanded you. And surely I am with you always, to
> the very end of the age.

This passage has become so familiar that we tend to miss the
depths to which it can take us in our day-to-day lives. As Jesus pre-
pares his disciples for his imminent departure, he is telling them
how to live. The disciples were wondering when Jesus was going to
return and what was going to happen (Acts 1:1–9). He tells them
he's leaving and is putting them in charge of his work!

Look closely at what he is saying. They are not called simply to preach the gospel. They are called to make disciples. He's not saying just to make converts. To become a disciple is not something simple, and he is telling them to make disciples of all nations, which is quite a job.

Verse 20 contains the most important point of this passage, which is that we, as believers, need to be taught and then teach others **to obey what Jesus has commanded.** That is how we become and make disciples. What are some things Jesus commanded?

Let's think back to Genesis 1:28 ". . . fill the earth and subdue it," "rule over . . . every living creature." Living what Christ commanded subdues a now fallen creation. Everything has been affected by the fall (Rom 8:18–23). To begin to change the impact it had, we must begin to subdue fallen creation through the Great Commission's mandate. We need to live good Great Commandment lives, purposefully obeying all that Jesus has commanded. There's a stark difference between what Jesus commanded and the rules that exist in the culture in which we live. When we commit to live out what he commanded, we begin to reclaim the culture, our relationships, our personal attitudes, and our values. We reclaim class and race along with everything that has fallen and is sin-laden, and we begin to renew that which has become imperfect.

Let's look at what Jesus commanded in Matthew 22:37–39 (NIV):

> Jesus replied: "'Love the Lord your God with all your heart and with all your soul and with all your mind.' This is the first and greatest commandment. And the second is like it: 'Love your neighbor as yourself.' All the Law and the Prophets hang on these two commandments."

God's purpose for our lives was and is for us to know him and to love him forever. His purpose for us has always been a relationship with him. When we love God with all our heart, soul, and mind, because of his indwelling Spirit and what Christ has done for us on the cross, we begin to reclaim the basic purpose he has for our lives. That purpose is to love him and to love others as we love ourselves. The Great Commandment is the impetus, motivation, and strength for everything else we do. When we understand that truth, we have the foundation to begin to live the purpose he has for us in all areas of our lives.

Let's turn now to Matthew 6:31–34 (NIV). At this point in Jesus' ministry, the disciples had been with him less than a year. They had left everything. They had left their families, and they were no doubt beginning to wonder how they were going to eat and get what they needed to live:

> So do not worry, saying, "What shall we eat?" or "What shall we drink?" or "What shall we wear?" For the pagans run after all these things, and your heavenly Father knows that you need them. But seek first his kingdom and his righteousness, and all these things will be given to you as well.
>
> Therefore do not worry about tomorrow, for tomorrow will worry about itself. Each day has enough trouble of its own.

Jesus is telling them to live "one day at a time." When we are empowered by the indwelling Spirit and living for Christ first, we begin to understand the power of his sovereignty and his presence in our lives. What ends up happening is that we have the ability, by God's grace, to look at our day-to-day struggles and difficulties and trust him. Once the relationship for which he created us forms and the trust occurs, we begin to have the peace that passes all understanding. We are human, and it is human to be anxious, but we begin to have peace in the midst of daily turmoil as we entrust our concerns to Christ. The more we walk closely with him, the greater the probability we won't be as anxious about life as we once were, and we will begin to reclaim the ability to experience internal peace. As we go forward and live in that peace, it has an effect on others as they see the difference in us compared to themselves.

What else can be said about what Jesus commanded? The story of the mother of James and John comes to mind. One day she approached Jesus and asked that when he came into his kingdom, would he have one of her sons sit at his right hand and the other at his left? She wanted places of prominence for her boys. The other disciples weren't present at the time, but when they found out what happened, an argument ensued, and they became indignant.

Here is what Jesus had to say in Matthew 20:26–28 (NIV) about what took place:

> Not so with you. Instead, whoever wants to become great among you must be your servant, and whoever wants to be first must be your slave—just as the Son of Man did not come to be served, but to serve, and to give his life as a ransom for many.

Jesus' disciples wanted prominence and position, yet he says he came to serve them, and that if they are truly his followers, it is their place to care for and serve others. In giving his disciples the Great Commission, Jesus directed them to replicate themselves by teaching others to "obey everything I have commanded you" which certainly includes the principles of Matthew 20:26–28. By following the principle of putting others first and serving them, we begin to use the proper approach toward other people instead of our natural, self-centered attitude. We then begin to reclaim relationships for him.

This is reinforced in Matthew 25:34–40 (NIV):

> "Then the King will say to those on his right, 'Come, you who are blessed by my Father; take your inheritance, the kingdom prepared for you since the creation of the world. For I was hungry and you gave me something to eat, I was thirsty and you gave me something to drink, I was a stranger and you invited me in, I needed clothes and you clothed me, I was sick and you looked after me, I was in prison and you came to visit me.'
>
> "Then the righteous will answer him, 'Lord, when did we see you hungry and feed you, or thirsty and give you something to drink? When did we see you a stranger and invite you in, or needing clothes and clothe you? When did we see you sick or in prison and go to visit you?'
>
> "The King will reply, 'I tell you the truth, whatever you did for one of the least of these brothers of mine, you did for me.'"

In this passage, Jesus separates the sheep and the goats, and we get a glimpse of what living as a servant serving the King of kings really looks like. As we care for the marginalized, we give dignity to all who are made in God's image. In that way, we help to reclaim humanity. As we implement that principle, the culture begins to change. It begins to look the way it would have looked or should have looked, and is a slight foretaste of what is to come.

There are many other things Jesus commanded and, as you can see, loving God totally and showing love and caring for others are paramount. This goes back to the Great Commandment. It does not go back to government, nor does it go back to societal norms. Imperfect people run government and society. As good as a government may be and as good as the people in positions of authority may be, government is manmade and as such is structured upon human perspective and understanding. Conversely, people who know Christ are inhabited by the third person of the Triune God. Their hearts have been changed and their perspectives are becoming different. They have been taught, and continue to learn, what Jesus has commanded.

What happens when we take seriously the call to obey everything Jesus has commanded? The culture, our piece of it, begins to change. We reclaim relationships and our individual purpose, our personal calling. In summary, being called is not only for those who are in vocational ministry. It is for all who have been called to Christ and therefore are called to be his ministers in every profession. Thus, by living his principles, values, ethics, and love in the world, the gospel becomes attractive to the world, and the world begins to change.

CHAPTER FIVE

Personal Spiritual Disciplines
Critical to Effective Ministry

THE NEXT FEW CHAPTERS will cover important truths I have learned (or am learning) over the past forty years. This chapter will address four that I believe are foundational to the life of a Christian, therefore making them critical for an effective ministry.

Prayer Needs to be the Foundation of All We Do

Several citations that support this are:

Matthew 26:36–39 (NIV)

> Then Jesus went with his disciples to a place called Gethsemane, and he said to them, "Sit here while I go over there and pray." He took Peter and the two sons of Zebedee along with him, and he began to be sorrowful and troubled. Then he said to them, "My soul is overwhelmed with sorrow to the point of death. Stay here and keep watch with me." Going a little farther, he fell with his face to the ground and prayed, "My Father, if it is possible, may this cup be taken from me. Yet not as I will, but as you will."

Mark 1:35–37 (NIV)

> Very early in the morning, while it was still dark, Jesus got up, left the house and went off to a solitary place, where he prayed. Simon and his companions went to look for him, and when they found him, they exclaimed: "Everyone is looking for you!"

Psalm 32:8 (NIV)

> I will instruct you and teach you in the way you should go; I will counsel you and watch over you.

Philippians 4:6–7 (NIV)

> Do not be anxious about anything, but in everything, by prayer and petition, with thanksgiving, present your requests to God. And the peace of God, which transcends all understanding, will guard your hearts and your minds in Christ Jesus.

James 1:5 (NIV)

> If any of you lacks wisdom, he should ask God, who gives generously to all without finding fault, and it will be given to him.

Ever since the end of 1974, when I began losing passion for my work and began sensing God leading me in a new direction, prayer has been an integral part of my life. Consequently, it has also been an integral part of Needle's Eye. As is the case with most Christian organizations, we send out prayer requests when people have illnesses, experience a tragic event, or are going through difficult times. However, several examples go beyond this. The first dates from the 1980s and into the early 1990s. It involved a group of ministers in Richmond from different denominations. All were committed to Christ and seeing his body, the church, transcend denominational barriers. It was a diverse group, including Pentecostals, Presbyterians, Baptists, Episcopalians, and Roman Catholics. Each of the individuals involved had a desire to pray for the city of Richmond. Among them were pastors, businessmen and women, and those involved in parachurch ministries such as

Needle's Eye. The desire arose because of the divisions that existed racially and even denominationally in the body of Christ in Richmond at that time.

The group initially met in an old church building in downtown Richmond located near what was the geographical center of the Richmond Metropolitan Region at the time. The group would gather on a Friday night and spend a couple of hours praying for Richmond, for the church, and for the group's individual ministries. It continued to meet periodically, and in the mid-1980s, began to set aside a Saturday morning each month when an even larger number of Christians would come together at one of a couple of storefront churches on Broad Street, the main street of downtown Richmond. Beyond church leaders, there were people from the Christian Medical and Dental Society, Needle's Eye, and World Horizons, an international outreach organization. Business people from other walks of life who cared about Richmond also came to join us.

Another example of our commitment to and dependence on prayer came about as a result of an association with David Bliss, a seminary colleague who worked with an organization in South Africa that had been involved in prayer initiatives throughout that country. They usually occurred on consecutive weekend days when a large segment of the body of Christ would come together and pray for their cities.

At our invitation, David came in March 1992 and led an event that was comprised of about seventy-five people. It began on a Friday night and continued through Saturday. A variety of churches and ministries from the inner city to the suburbs were represented. Subsequently, there were prayer meetings that met on the second Saturday morning of the month through 1992 with a late afternoon planning meeting in our offices the preceding Thursday.

In January 1993, Andrew Fuller—the North American Director of World Horizons—and I met to pray and plan. This led to three more spring meetings resulting in a steering committee being formed to give direction to a citywide concert of prayer to be held the following fall. The Second Saturday Prayer Meetings continued, recruiting and promotion began, and excitement began to build.

On November 9, 1993, David Bryant, a well-known prayer warrior and leader of Concerts of Prayer, an interdenominational ministry based in New York, led us in a citywide prayer meeting. Needle's Eye spearheaded this event and well over sixty churches and sponsoring ministries were involved.

A good deal of effort went into spreading the word and preparing for the concert, and God blessed our efforts. Held on a Friday night at the Arthur Ashe Center, a multipurpose arena in Richmond, more than 800 were in attendance. It was a wonderful depiction of the body of Christ including all denominations, ages, races, and backgrounds.

Follow-up meetings were incorporated into the Second Saturday Prayer Meetings and attendance swelled (sixty-seven one month). Additionally, a monthly pastors' meeting was convened. These meetings took place in churches in the suburbs, city, and inner city projects. Among those represented were Episcopal, Baptist, Presbyterian, African Methodist Episcopal, Assemblies of God, Christian and Missionary Alliance, Lutheran, Roman Catholic, and non-denominational churches, as well as a Messianic Jewish synagogue. These prayer gatherings continued through the summer of 1997. The Second Saturday Prayer Meetings continued through September 2000.

Somewhat concurrent with these meetings, the National Day of Prayer (the first Thursday in May) started in Richmond in 1995. This effort was facilitated by Dr. James Anderson, a local physician who had been working behind the scenes for years to promote reconciliation, healing, and unity in the body of Christ in Richmond. Subsequent to the first National Day of Prayer gathering, Dr. Anderson and his colleagues sponsored two pastors' conferences in 1996 and 1997. These conferences resulted in a monthly pastors' prayer meeting that crossed racial, denominational, and ethnic lines. It lasted for ten years and led to quarterly prayer meetings that incorporated some of our community leaders.

In 2005, we began having bi-monthly prayer meetings at Needle's Eye. These soon became monthly and still continue today. This is an opportunity for what we call our core to come together and pray. This includes our Board of Directors, Advisory Board, Directors' Council, Pastors' Council, Christian Presidents Groups, and small group leaders. These individuals have the opportunity to come to our office in the middle of a workday during their lunch hour. They pray for the needs and concerns of specific individuals connected to Needle's Eye, new outreaches underway, ministry decisions that need to be made, the needs of family members, and so forth.

Those previously-mentioned quarterly prayer meetings ultimately spawned "Bless Richmond" in 2011. This movement was a conglomerate of churches representing all sizes, ethnicities, and denominations. Bless Richmond was committed to caring for the poor and disenfranchised, and to reconciliation and unity within the body of Christ in Richmond. For six years Bless Richmond sponsored a citywide prayer and worship service attended by thousands. The nonrequired "ticket" to the event was canned goods which were donated to the Central Virginia Food Bank. Needle's Eye participated in these events, and we witnessed the Lord using them in wonderful ways.

Consistent and ongoing prayer is critical for individuals, a ministry, and a community. It keeps us plugged into the One who is actually in charge. When a new outreach, decision, or direction is under consideration, we always take it to the Lord in prayer. We have been richly blessed! God has consistently answered our prayers and provided the direction we needed. He is more than faithful!

Trust God to Meet All of Our Needs

The next spiritual discipline for this discussion is to trust God. Two of many biblical citations that support this are:

Proverbs 3:5–6 (NIV)

> Trust in the Lord with all your heart and lean not on your own understanding; in all your ways acknowledge him, and he will make your paths straight.

Philippians 4:19 (NIV)

> And my God will meet all your needs according to his glorious riches in Christ Jesus.

Deuteronomy and Hebrews, remind us that God will never fail or forsake us. The difficulty is that we regularly forsake him.

Ultimately, rather than putting our faith in our investment portfolios, careers, or networks of business contacts, we must trust God to meet our needs. It's true, however, that God does use people in support of our needs. I'll relate a few examples.

We returned home to Richmond in June 1977, the month following my graduation from Gordon-Conwell. We very much wanted to find a rental house in the school district in which we had lived before moving to Massachusetts. We were not optimistic, however. We thought it would be virtually impossible, because rental houses in that area were rare, especially houses we could afford.

As anticipated, there were no rental houses advertised the first few days of Laura's house-hunting trip, just prior to graduation. Both our home in Richmond and the rental house in Massachusetts had nice child-friendly yards, and Laura was having a difficult time mentally dealing with going back to apartment living. She prayed faithfully, began looking at apartment options, and got to the point of accepting it as God's apparent will for us at this time.

Once she had fully accepted it, everything changed. God was faithful, and, as you know, with him all things are possible. The next day a rental house we could afford came on the market in that school district and an ad for it appeared in the newspaper. She had an interview with the owner, and the house was ours if we wanted it. It was a small three-bedroom, one-bath ranch. When the owner opened the utility room, he apologized for the extra toilet there.

With two boys, Laura was just thrilled there was a second one, and it didn't have to be fancy. She immediately committed to the rental, and we were so thankful! We were thrilled to be back in the school district we had chosen for our children before we had any idea we would be leaving town and going to seminary. God knew that was the desire of our hearts and he honored it. He is so good!

Needle's Eye officially began on July 1, 1977, with less than $3,000 on hand. Money was tight. We were living hand-to-mouth, week-to-week. I cannot remember receiving two full salary checks back-to-back until 1979. Even so, we knew God would provide because we believed he had called us to this ministry and, of course, he did. One day in December 1977, Laura sat down to pay bills after I'd left for the office. She looked at the checkbook, and then at the list of bills that were due. They totaled $400 and fifty dollars was in the account. She thought, "Lord, it's going to be really interesting to see how you work this one out."

Twenty minutes later, the doorbell rang. A man was at the door who had contributed to us when we were in seminary.

"Is Buddy here?"

"No, he's gone to the office."

Handing her a check, he said, "My wife and I were praying last night, and we believe God was leading us to give you this. Please give it to Buddy when he comes home."

I have shared this story a number of times and each time I do, I ask the question, "How much do you think the check was for?" Most everyone says $400. No, it was for $350, the exact amount needed to cover those bills.

There were so many other amazing examples of how the Lord met our many needs. Among them were the gift of a downpayment for our first post-seminary home, cars being provided when our family cars were no longer functioning, other cars periodically being gifted for ministry use, medical and dental care being provided to our entire family, vacation homes being shared with us, and the home in which we continue to live being built for us at cost. By his grace, we were trusting God to meet all our needs.

Here's another example. Before returning to Richmond, I was thinking quite a lot about how to roll out the ministry. However, I failed to consider a few practical issues with which I needed to deal, such as the need for an office. I just assumed I'd have to work out of my home, a small ranch-style house. When I'd been in Richmond the summer before my final year of seminary, I met a man named Sam Jackson, a well-known executive with a large corporation who also owned numerous investment properties. After arriving back in Richmond in June 1977, Sam gave me a call.

"Do you want to work out of your house?" he asked.

"No," I said.

"Do you want an office?"

"No."

Sam said, "I don't understand."

"I don't want to work out of my house," I said, "but I can't afford an office."

"Oh, I see," Sam said. "Do you think you can afford twenty dollars a month?"

"I don't know, Sam, maybe." Yes, that was actually my response, because things were so tight!

"Tell you what. I own a building that has a small office. I'd let you have it for free, but I just did that a year ago for someone from Young Life. My partner won't let me do it again, so I have to charge something. I'd like you to try to pay me twenty dollars a month."

Trust God! He provided an office for twenty dollars a month, a godsend because at home there were two young, active children and one on the way. Needless to say, it would have been hard to get anything accomplished. The office was in the basement of Sam's building, but it had its own entrance down some steps from the outside, where a few trashcans were positioned nearby. The room had a sink on the wall, the toilet was in the closet, and the heat pipes for the entire building went through the room. No charm included, but because of that pipe, my heating bills were ridiculously low. What a blessing!

That little office worked well for Needle's Eye for about four years, but as time went by, our work expanded. I hired a part-time employee for a position which later became full time. Sam was able to provide us an additional small room next to my office, but we had to go outside to get to one another's space.

The ministry continued to grow, and God surprised me by using an old business acquaintance to help take us to the next level. Prior to and during my seminary years, a charismatic renewal was sweeping the country. It started on the West Coast and moved east and south. Many came to faith during that time, including a businessman I knew in Richmond named Phil McKown. I'd met Phil when I was in college and working part time in my dad's printing business. Phil owned two businesses, one of which was somewhat of a competitor to my dad's. He and I became reacquainted when I returned to Richmond, and we grew to be close friends once we found that the other had come to Christ. Phil sold his businesses in 1981 and joined us as a volunteer, doing bookkeeping, administrative work, and individual ministry with business people. By this time, we had rented a third disconnected one-room office from Sam. We'd get wet going to one another's offices if it was raining. As you can imagine, this set-up was even more challenging!

The Lord solved that issue in 1981, once again providing for our growing needs. One day I was in my office getting ready for a counseling session, and Phil walked in.

"What are you doing?" he said.

"Getting ready for a counseling session I have in less than an hour."

"Come with me," Phil said.

"But I have a counseling session and preparation to do."

"Come on. It won't take long."

"Okay, but you've got to have me back here in thirty minutes."

We got into Phil's car, and he drove less than two miles to a duplex.

"A realtor friend is here," Phil said. "I want you to walk through this with us and tell me if you like it."

It was great! It had one and a half bathrooms, neither of which was in a closet, a basement conference room, and two additional floors with six rooms.

"Sure I like it," I said, "but I can't afford it!"

"I didn't ask if you could afford it," Phil said. "I asked if you like it."

"Well, sure," I said.

"Here's the deal. I'm going to buy it for the ministry. All I want you to do is try to make the mortgage payments."

"How much will they be?" I asked.

"Oh, about $650."

"I'll try."

And we did! God used Phil as a conduit to provide a much-needed larger and nicer office, and we didn't even need a capital campaign to try to raise the money.

As you might suspect, we grew to fill that space. Fast-forward to 1997, we had four paid staff members and two volunteers. Again, space was cramped. We had started holding a number of small group sessions each week and all we had to hold them in was a small conference room in the basement. We were also sharing office space with the Christian Counseling and Training Center ministry, which we had started in 1982. So we began looking for another building.

I really liked the area we were in because it was centrally located and near the entrance and exit to the expressway. I could be anywhere in about fifteen minutes or less, and the street was fairly quiet and had a sense of privacy about it. Business people felt at ease about coming to our office for counseling, a small group meeting, or other types of ministry.

A building across the street was available, but it had a flat roof. During the time we'd been there, I'd seen that building's roof repaired or replaced three times!

"What about that building?" people would ask.

My answer was always, "I don't want a flat-roofed building!"

Four businessmen constituents of ours became a self-appointed group to find a new building. They looked, I looked, and none of us could find anything. Finally, they said, you like this location, and there's nothing available except the building across the street with the flat roof. We can probably afford that building. Why don't you pray about it?

So I did pray about it, and before long we began negotiating with the owners. The self-appointed committee led a charge that raised the money for Needle's Eye to buy the building. We paid cash, although we did have to finance a $60,000 renovation because we decided to remove a load-bearing wall in order to create two conference rooms now used daily for small group meetings. That loan was repaid in less than a year. As I write this twenty years later, we are still in the building. Although it may not be an architectural masterpiece, it has served our needs well.

You are probably wondering about the roof. During our first year in the building, one of our constituents put a plastic overlay on it at no cost to us. In the past twenty years, there have been only two occasions when we have had to have the roof patched.

In 2003, a current board member and long-time donor took a hard look at our cash flow pattern. He noted that donations dropped off significantly in the summer from June to September and then again in February. He knew this almost always put a squeeze on us. He blessed us by donating $350,000, the proceeds from the sale of a piece of land, to Needle's Eye. The purpose of the gift was to create an emergency fund that would cover the shortfalls which typically occurred. This was a blessing! We would, for example, take out $20,000 in August to cover expenses when income was low, and then replace the money in October or November. If we had not had that money during the Great Recession of 2008 to 2010, I do not know what we would have done.

In May 2008, we had hired a small group coordinator—our first. At that time we had about twenty-five small groups, and our strategic plan called for expansion. As a result, we were looking for a larger building. In August, we began negotiations for one with more than twice the space we had. Before long, we were ready to make an offer. I called the owner and told him he would be receiving one and that it was going to require ninety days due diligence, because we had concerns about asbestos and possibly other issues. If everything worked out, and we certainly thought it would, we were going to buy the building.

The owner said he would not accept an offer with a ninety-day contingency. He had another potential buyer who was willing to pay cash and needed no contingencies. He'd like to see an offer from us, of course, but would not entertain the ninety day stipulation. I told him the amount of our offer, which I thought he would find attractive, but said we had to have ninety days. He turned us down, and we were definitely very disappointed.

That happened at the end of August 2008. The cost of the building would have been about $1.5 million. Sixty days later the stock market cratered. If the offer had gone through, we would have been trying to raise $1.5 million at a time when virtually every potential donor was experiencing serious financial difficulty. Trust God to meet all your needs, whether or not you know you have them!

By the fall of 2009, donations had dropped off dramatically. I went to several of our significant donors because we were using up that fund rapidly. I explained we had an emergency fund that had started out at $300,000 ($50,000 was a deferred payment) and was now down to about $150,000. I was concerned! Some of these gentlemen served on boards other than mine and knew what was going on around town. They were quick to tell me that Needle's Eye, with this fund, was much better off than most other nonprofits. Not only were our needs being met, we still had money in the bank, which was not the case for many.

Obedience is Critical but Doesn't Always Equate With Comfort

Acts 5:29–30, 33 (NIV):

> Peter and the other apostles replied: "We must obey God rather than men!" "The God of our fathers raised Jesus from the dead—whom you killed by hanging him on a tree." . . . "When they heard this, they were furious and wanted to put them to death."

1 John 2:17

> The world and its desires pass away, but the man who
> does the will of God lives forever.

In the Great Commission in Matthew 28:19–20, Jesus says to "make disciples of all the nations, baptizing them in the name of the Father and the Son and the Holy Spirit, teaching them to obey all that I commanded you." This makes it clear: obedience is critical for every believer. This is difficult for us because obedience is not in our nature. Our nature has always been to want to be our own god. As you know, it only took three chapters in the first book of the Bible for that to surface.

In 1982, we'd been in ministry five years, and the Billy Graham Evangelistic Association was going strong. Every year that organization would select three or four of the crusade sites in North America to hold what they called The Billy Graham School of Evangelism in conjunction with the crusade. The crusade would take place each evening for a week, and during each weekday ministers would be provided with ongoing education in evangelism. I went to one of these in Boston and can testify that there were outstanding speakers for about six hours every day.

The Billy Graham School of Evangelism was also an incredible gift to young ministers. The School would pay your travel expenses and put you up in a hotel. Your only expense was your food. The only requirement was that you had to go to the crusade every night—and grade the preacher! Of course, the preacher was always the same, Billy Graham, so there was never much doubt about the grade.

The last presentation on the last day of school was given by Leighton Ford, Billy Graham's brother-in-law. Dr. Ford had his own ministry which was evangelistically oriented and focused on raising up young leaders to spread the message of Christ. His talk was on the concept of being bold for Christ. While he was speaking, I was impressed with the fact that God was leading us to be bold in Richmond. We would go into churches at noontime and put a businessman or woman in front of 100 or more people to talk about how Jesus had changed their lives. Nevertheless, that still small voice was telling me we needed to be even more bold. It seemed that God wanted us to do outdoor preaching to business and professional people in Richmond. As this became clear, I was startled. I didn't want to do it! I eventually told the Lord, "Lord, you just don't evangelize white-collar people like that! It would turn them off." God, however, did not relent. By the time Leighton Ford was finished, I was convicted that what I was hearing was in fact what God wanted, and I was very unsettled.

I struggled with this for months. Finally, I took the idea to my Board of Directors and told them I felt God leading us to do outdoor preaching. I also told them I thought we were to do it on the grounds of the Virginia State Capitol. As a native of Richmond, who as a businessman previously had his office downtown, I knew that in the summer, on a nice day, business people would get a lunch and go to that lovely and peaceful place to eat it. The grounds were like a park in the middle of downtown Richmond, and a couple hundred people would come and go during lunch hour each weekday. The board thought I had lost my mind, and that didn't surprise me. It took almost a year for us to get on the same page.

I had gone to seminary with Cliff Knechtle, a man who had played Division I basketball for Lefty Driesell at Davidson University. When Cliff finished seminary, he went with InterVarsity as a campus preacher and was already doing outdoor preaching. I was on his mailing list and saw that he was going to be at the University of Virginia. That was in March 1984. I called Cliff and told him about my Leighton Ford experience, my Board of Directors' reaction, and my initial reluctance. I asked him what he thought. Cliff said it was obvious that God wanted me to do it!

After confirming the time and place that Cliff was going to be at the University of Virginia, I told him I wanted to come to Charlottesville to watch him in action. He said that would be great.

The day arrived, and I stood at the back of an outdoor crowd of about 200. Cliff came to the podium, made a few introductory remarks, and then said, "A friend of mine is here today. He has driven all the way from Richmond. Before I begin, he would like to say a few words."

I was shocked, unprepared, and stunned! We had not talked about my speaking, only observing. However, this experience solidified in my mind that outdoor preaching was what God wanted us to do. To make a long story short, our board agreed unanimously to pursue outdoor preaching at the Capitol. We secured a permit, borrowed a sound system, and began a series of annual, weeklong outreaches on the grounds of the Virginia State Capitol. This ministry continued for five years. I don't believe we ever had less than 150 to 200 people, and topped out at just over 500. I have never been more nervous in my life than I was before I preached that first day. However, by God's grace, once I opened my mouth, I was never nervous again about preaching outdoors. After the first year, our format was local pastors and ministry leaders who would preach Mondays through Thursdays, and I would wrap up the week on Fridays. We had a common theme each week, and each preacher would have his elders, deacons, or vestry members stationed on the corners of downtown Richmond handing out fliers during the lunch hour announcing the next week's speaker. People actually came to faith in Jesus Christ during those outdoor preaching event days!

Allow me to give you another example of being obedient and uncomfortable. In the mid-1990s, we had prayerfully spent some time on strategic planning, were looking for a new building, and felt called to do some cultural sensitization to prime the pump for the gospel in Metro Richmond, things like radio spots and perhaps articles or newspaper ads. I went to a business owner who had been giving us a fairly significant gift annually and told him of our plan, that we needed more space, and wanted to do some cultural sensitization. He liked the idea and asked how much it would cost. I said we were thinking of producing radio spots and running them on secular stations, which would cost in the neighborhood of $30,000 to $50,000. I also told him of our need for additional office space. He said he couldn't do the building part right now and preferred to wait until we had a building in mind and knew the cost. Although he could have done the radio spots immediately, his preference was to fund them both together. He was willing to donate the money for the radio spots then, but I suggested we wait until he felt more secure about what he could give and was in a position to do both. When I told my board chairman what I'd done, he thought I'd lost my mind for not taking what I could get right then.

This board chairman, one of my closest friends, was all in on this entire project. He was consistently available to me, making personal calls himself to raise money for the building. One such call was on a friend of his who had fairly recently become involved with Needle's Eye. My friend became a bit reluctant and uneasy when he discovered that this individual was actually of the opinion that we should rent a building, rather than buy. My chairman asked him to further pray about the situation and left thinking it had been an awful call and that he would never hear from him again. Several days later, he called my chairman and asked, "Would $100,000 help?" My chairman had been obedient and God had done the rest! From the two donors who were approached, we ultimately received gifts that met and exceeded expectations. In each of these instances we were able to clearly see the hand of God at work. In my former life as a salesman, I would normally give serious consideration to any reasonable deal on the table. By God's sovereignty, I declined to accept the first donor's original offer. My chairman, working as hard as he could for Needle's Eye, thought he had failed in his attempt to secure the significant gift from the second. In each case, trusting the Lord's principles and being obedient to him resulted in our needs being met, his will being done, and his Son being glorified.

Now let's return to the radio spots. We produced five radio spots which ran for about three months, and later ran again for another three to four weeks. They were incredible! In fact, one of them won 3rd Place in the New York Festival of Radio Advertising. Another that aired just before Easter is what caused my discomfort. It featured a man who had just closed a big sale and was calling his wife from the car to tell her about it. He shared excitedly how they would soon have plenty of money, that she would be able to renovate the kitchen, etc. All of a sudden, there was the sound of tires squealing and glass breaking, and the man was killed. The message, of course, was that we never know when our number will come up and our time on earth will end. The announcer then read John 3:16, "For God so loved the world that he gave his one and only Son, that whoever believes in him shall not perish but have eternal life."

That spot ran less than five days before one station took it off the air. The radio station's phone was ringing off the hook with women calling because they were picturing their husbands dying in a car wreck. We had been obedient to God, and done what we were led to do, but I have to say the cancellation of that spot made me uncomfortable. Even so, the Richmond community was so impacted by those spots that, even after twenty years, I still hear comments about that radio campaign.

Another example of obedience not equating with comfort started in 2001. From an article in the *Richmond Times–Dispatch,* I learned about an outreach effort to young people in Northern Virginia. The Roman Catholic diocese had a program underway called Theology on Tap.

I thought, "Wow. Theology on Tap! What an incredibly awesome name, particularly for spiritual seekers."

We went to investigate that outreach two times. The first was with my board chairman, the one who'd been frustrated I hadn't taken the radio money when it was offered. On the second trip we took six board members. Both times we saw about 250 young people, all under the age of thirty, gathered together in a bar—one in the District of Columbia and the other in Arlington.

The objective of the program was to bring young Catholics back into the fold after college. A priest would talk for fifteen or twenty minutes, followed by a question-and-answer session. As this was going on, people stood watching and listening attentively while they relaxed after work with a beer. You could have heard a pin drop as the message was being delivered!

After those visits, we felt this was a great opportunity to reach young people in the Richmond business community and that God was leading us to do it. All we needed was to find a place within walking distance of a business community where young people would like to hang out on a weekday after work. We wanted to call it Theology on Tap but couldn't because the name was trademarked. Our outreach became Spiritual Shots. We had a logo created for it with a beer bottle top replacing the "O" in Shots. The tag line was, "The Best Buzz in Richmond." It was a little edgy, but just what we needed to reach the younger crowd.

Well, as you might expect, we had several church leaders call and say, "If you do what you are planning to do, we are going to pull your funding." One of our long-time supporters flew off the handle because of the tagline. I explained the double entendre, "buzz" meant "positive word of mouth," and he said he knew it meant that, and he also knew it meant something else. As a result of that initial negative reaction, I told the board we might lose some money, but frankly I didn't care. Jesus had done the same sort of thing. He drank with prostitutes and tax collectors. He was called a drunkard even though he never got drunk. I said if God is leading us to do this, and I believe he is, we will be okay. The board agreed.

The program began in 2001 at a restaurant called Havana 59, and we later moved it to Bottoms Up Pizza, located in the Shockoe Bottom district within walking distance of downtown Richmond. Several contributors did pull their funding (although one later returned), but the Spiritual Shots outreach program was a big success and lasted a total of fifteen years. Sometimes being obedient is not comfortable, but it is always the best course to take.

Listen to the Spirit

The final point of this chapter is to listen to the Spirit. Among the biblical citations that support this are:

John 16:13 (NIV)

> But when he, the Spirit of truth, comes, he will guide you into all truth. He will not speak on his own; he will speak only what he hears, and he will tell you what is yet to come.

1 Corinthians 2:10–13 (NIV)

> but God has revealed it to us by his Spirit. The Spirit searches all things, even the deep things of God. For who

among men knows the thoughts of a man except the man's spirit within him? In the same way no one knows the thoughts of God except the Spirit of God. We have not received the spirit of the world but the Spirit who is from God, that we may understand what God has freely given us. This is what we speak, not in words taught us by human wisdom but in words taught by the Spirit, expressing spiritual truths in spiritual words.

In Chapter 1, I explained that about a year after I accepted Jesus Christ as my Lord and Savior, I lost the passion I'd had for my work. This was a big change for me, and I gathered a group of men to give me input and support me in prayer. That's the way many determine God's will—by gathering a band of brothers or sisters together who love the Lord and love you, asking them to pray for you and to give input. That way, they become a conduit for God.

As you know, all in the group around me agreed God was leading me to go to seminary. I had a difficult time with that at first because it was a discipline in which I had no background. It was hard getting my head around the idea, but the more I met with the group and the more I prayed about it, the more it seemed to be the right direction. Even so, I was reluctant.

One in the group asked me, "Do you want Christ to drive the car of your life?"

I said, "Yes, I do."

"Well, then, what you need to do is get out from behind the wheel."

"Okay, but how?" I asked.

"You need to take some steps."

"What steps?"

"Take action. Look at seminaries. Apply to some."

I began thinking and praying about that. I'd been a follower of Christ for a little more than a year at the time, and even though I was a new believer, the church I was attending put me on a board that was the equivalent of the Board of Deacons in the Baptist tradition or the vestry in the Episcopal church. Then something totally unexpected happened. I heard a voice when driving home alone one night following one of those meetings. It was the first time this had happened to me. The voice seemed to come from the backseat, and said loud and clear, "I want you in my ministry."

I turned to see who was there, ran off the road and part way up an embankment. I turned the wheel and, thankfully, was able to get the car back on the road—all the while wondering what was going on.

Five seconds later the voice again said, "I want you in my ministry."

As you can imagine, this made a significant impact on me, and I began to seriously pursue the possibility of going to seminary.

Let me say that by listening to the Spirit I'm not suggesting it will always be an audible voice, or even that still small voice. However this time, and a couple of other times, it has been for me.

Here is another story about listening to the Spirit. In my second semester of seminary, after we had decided to pursue a ministry to business and professional people, I was in a class taught by my advisor. This particular day he got off track and onto a point that did not have anything to do with the day's lecture. There were thirty or so ministers-to-be in the room, and he said, "What I am about to tell you is something you are going to struggle with your whole life."

This got our attention.

"You would not be here," he said, "unless you felt God wanted you to go into vocational ministry. You will always struggle with this because you will equate your personal relationship with Christ to your work. All of your life, you are going to struggle with putting your work on par with your relationship with him, and let me tell you—that is not God's will!"

He told the class to turn to 1 Timothy 3. The first part of that chapter talks about elders. He then said this text lists the requirements for leadership in the church. Verses 2–4, and 6–7 are about overseers [elders] and verses 8–10 and 12 refer to deacons. Many attributes apply to both including being worthy of respect, being honest, not given to drunkenness, and each must manage his children and household well."

He then focused on verse 5, which states, "If anyone does not know how to manage his own family, how can he take care of God's church?" The professor said, "Do you see what this text is saying? It's saying that if you are a leader of the church, the first priority is to have your own home in order. That means that next to your personal relationship with Christ, your family comes before your work—even if your work is for him!"

This was a revelation to me. As you know, before I came to Christ, number one in my life was work and what it could provide in terms of money and prestige. Now my life had changed—the superficial as well as some of the important things. My marriage was good, and I was sensitive about being a good father, but I was not spending much time at home. Because I was in a discipline in which I had no background before seminary, I went to the library every night. Even before I went to seminary, if I found out about a Bible study or a prayer and praise meeting, I was there, because all of this was so incredibly new and exciting to me. So there I was, listening to my advisor talking about priorities. I was thinking my life had changed, but what he was talking about was definitely not in my thought process. This was new—this idea that my family was *that* important—even more important than work for God!

I began to think about and process this, and it percolated for a few weeks or so before something happened that I will never forget. When I came home each evening, I'd have dinner, then go to a library at a college about a mile away, Merrimack College in North Andover, Massachusetts. One night I was there studying for the next day's mid-term exam on Paul and his Letters, all thirteen of them! It was a big, significant mid-term, covering a lot of material.

All of a sudden, I heard a voice say, "Are you going to trust me?"

I always studied in the same carrel, and the same young man usually sat in the one behind me. I looked back, thinking he was playing with me, but his head was buried in a book. I turned back to my studies.

A minute or so later, the voice again said, "Are you going to trust me?"

This time, I knew what the voice was. It was God asking if I was going to trust him and his principles, or if I was going to stay behind the wheel.

I looked at my watch. It was about seven o'clock. I packed up, drove home, and arrived before the kids had gone to bed. Laura gave me a strange look.

"What are you doing home?" she asked.

I said, "I just wanted to come home and help you put the kids to bed." Later, I told her about my experience in the library.

The next day in the exam, concepts came to me I hadn't thought about before, and I put them down on paper. Miraculously, I did well on that exam.

Hearing an audible voice never happened to me again, but the principle of listening to the Spirit, in whatever manner, has stayed with me for more than forty years. I believe it, I know it, and I teach this principle whenever I have the opportunity. I listened to the Spirit, in this case an audible voice, and it helped me align my life priorities with his.

For me and for most people I know, hearing the Spirit as an actual voice is unusual. Most often, the Spirit speaks to us in more subtle ways. For example, as discussed in chapter 1, following two weeks of devotions and prayer for guidance, Laura and I came to understand I was being called to minister to business and professional people. That is another way of listening to and hearing the Spirit—through Scripture, quiet time, and through others, including my wife and my seminary advisor.

Here's my final story about listening to the Spirit. In 1982, Needle's Eye had been going for five years. God had shown favor to the ministry and had led me to meet a number of business and professional people, some of whom were very successful. However, even though I had been called to minister to the white-collar crowd, I could not get over the number of homeless people in Richmond. They seemed to be multiplying. One man hung around my office, and I'd bring him in out of the weather from time to time, especially during the winter.

As I have mentioned repeatedly, the Great Commission is to "make disciples of all nations," (Matt 28:19) and it's done by obeying what God has told us to do. Some of the things Jesus said were counterintuitive, such as "Don't worry about tomorrow," (Matt

6:34) and "instead, whoever wants to become great among you must be your servant, and whoever wants to be first must be your slave" (Matt 20:26–27). Matthew 25:36–40 is one of the most significant passages in this regard:

> "I needed clothes and you clothed me, I was sick and you looked after me, I was in prison and you came to visit me." Then the righteous will answer him, "Lord, when did we see you hungry and feed you, or thirsty and give you something to drink? When did we see you a stranger and invite you in, or needing clothes and clothe you? When did we see you sick or in prison and go to visit you?" The King will reply, "I tell you the truth, whatever you did for one of the least of these brothers of mine, you did for me."

Because of these truths, it seemed to me that we, as a ministry primarily to the white-collar community, had a great opportunity. God had blessed our constituency not just financially, but with gifts and abilities. The gifts they possessed, and what they could offer in addition to money, were—and are—desperately needed by the poor. This is Discipleship 101, allowing God to use the gifts he has given us in the lives of others. This thought at times almost consumed my thinking, and I couldn't shake it. Finally, it became clear that our constituency needed the opportunity to focus on giving what God had given them to those who needed and could not afford it. There was never an audible voice—just a continually growing sense that it was what God wanted, and he was not going to relent until we took action.

Out of that began what was called the CrossOver Ministry. Today, it is known as CrossOver Healthcare Ministry, the largest nonprofit health clinic to the underprivileged in Virginia and a perfect example of the child outgrowing the parent. There are half a dozen or so medical professionals on the payroll, and a staff of about forty, and they have more than 6,000 patient visits a year. This ministry came into being as a direct result of listening to and being prodded by the Spirit.

CHAPTER SIX

Foundational Truths on Which to Build a Ministry

IN CHAPTER 5, WE covered personal spiritual disciplines that are critical to effective ministry. We will discuss foundational truths upon which to build a ministry in chapter 6. As the narrative unfolds, reflect on how the spiritual disciplines either directly or indirectly support or interweave with these foundational truths.

Unanimity in Board Decision-Making

From the beginning, the board of Needle's Eye has operated under the principle that board decisions should be unanimous. Although this may not be the case for every Christian organization, and certainly there are many examples in Scripture where this has not been the case, it is what we believe God directed us to do.

You may recall that I spent the summer before my final year at Gordon-Conwell in Richmond, and during that time the original Needle's Eye board was established. The following spring, as I was finishing the last few months prior to graduation, I received a telephone call from one of the board members. I'd just returned from a meeting in Richmond with potential supporters. The board member said he had been thinking about how we ought to operate and was wondering what would happen if, as a board, we ever came to a point when we did not agree. He said, for example, that I might want to go in one direction, and some on the board might believe a different direction was better. What would happen then?

I thought about it briefly and realized that I would be involved day-to-day in the ebb and flow of ministry. In my thinking, the board's role was to be a sounding board and to give encouragement, direction, and advice. It seemed to me that if a critical decision had to be made, it should fall to me to make it, and that is what I told my board member.

He said, "Oh," and nothing more.

I asked him if he wanted to talk about it further, and he said it was something we would eventually need to discuss.

That exchange and his question began to bother me. It occurred to me that God might be trying to say something to me through this board member. A day or two later, I talked to my advisor, Dr. Wilson, about it. I explained the conversation, my initial thinking, and my concern about my board member's reaction.

Dr. Wilson said, "So we are talking about decision making at the board level for Needle's Eye, right?"

"Yes, that's right."

"Buddy, I've never known God to be divided on any issue, have you?"

The truth of that comment was undeniable, and I said so.

Dr. Wilson said, "Then it seems to me, decision-making by the Needle's Eye Board ought to be based on unanimity."

That was all it took. From then on, unanimity was the way it was going to be.

Allow me to give an example of how that has worked. In the early 1980s, we were considering a woman involved with Needle's Eye for board membership. She had been involved in several of our outreaches, and I had become enthusiastic about her and had put her name forward.

At the time, we had seven or eight board members, and it was, of course, impossible for all of them to intimately know everyone who was involved with the ministry. A couple of people on the board said they wanted to get to know her before they voted, and we tabled the discussion. At the next meeting, following discussion we tabled it again. At the third meeting all but one were ready to vote. If we had, the result would have been seven for and one against.

The board member who was opposed said, "I'm sorry, but I just cannot vote for her. I don't really know her, but even so, I just have this sense that it would not be the right decision."

Because of our unanimity principle, we moved on. Within two months, a story became public that demonstrated without a doubt that the board member who would not vote for her had been correct. He had been used by God to keep us on track.

Another example has to do with the budgeting process. Although we now have a pastors' council with eighteen or so churches represented, for the most part our board is comprised of business people. When they look at numbers and budgets, they tend to look at them differently than most who are in vocational ministry. Our fiscal year begins on July 1st. We typically look at budgets in May and then vote on them in June.

Over the years, there have been several times when we didn't get a budget passed on time. As a result, I have found that if you have to wait on someone with whom you disagree, a level of grace and civility can begin to grow. When it does, the trust level ratchets up. When there is trust, the ability to see the other's perspective increases as does sensitivity to one another. I have seen this dynamic often. Although frustrating at times, unanimity in board decisions has been a blessing to us. I encourage others to prayerfully consider adopting this practice.

Have a Kingdom Mindset

This foundational truth obviously makes sense because the body of Christ is much bigger than any church, denomination, or movement. An opportunity to put this truth to work arose in the late 1980s when a program was developed that involved a number of churches of different denominations, geographic locations, ethnicities, and racial backgrounds. It was called Opportunity in October. Over the course of a week, a number of pastors worked together to take the message of salvation through Jesus Christ to church congregations and their surrounding communities throughout the metropolitan area.

Seven churches were involved, representing five denominations. Pastors of churches from all four major geographic sectors of Richmond preached each evening during the week, but they did not preach at their home churches. For example, a West End pastor from a suburban upscale neighborhood might preach at a church located in a government housing project in the East End, a Presbyterian Church in America (PCA) pastor might preach in an Assemblies of God church, and an inner-city pastor might preach in an Episcopal church. The pastors, preaching on the same predetermined theme each night, rotated to different churches every evening over the course of the week. Consequently, congregations in each church would receive the same message every night, but that message would come from the perspective of a different pastor. We did not have a formal way to measure results, but I can say, based on anecdotal evidence, that the results appeared to have been significant, not only to the church congregations, but most certainly to the pastors.

Another example is an effort mentioned in the previous chapter called Concerts of Prayer. Soon after I returned from Gordon-Conwell, there seemed to be a desire in Richmond churches to reach out beyond traditional denominational, geographic, and racial barriers in order to bring the body of Christ together. You may recall I wrote earlier about a prayer meeting around 1980 that blossomed into an ongoing affair. This initial meeting took place in Monumental Church in downtown Richmond.

Much later, in 1993, Needle's Eye initiated a collective effort to bring David Bryant, a man known internationally for conducting what were called Concerts of Prayer. The goal of these gatherings was to bring an entire community, with all of its diversity, together for an evening of directed prayer for the needs of the Christian community and those of the metropolitan region in general. Approximately sixty churches and parachurch ministries throughout the area were involved. The result was that more than 800 people attended, prayed, and worshipped together for over three hours. It was a wonderful experience and a foretaste, I believe, of what heaven will be like.

Another example also comes from the early 1990s when we established what we call our Pastors' Council, which currently represents eighteen churches from about ten different denominations. We look to the Pastors' Council to be a source of feedback and input. It helps to keep us on track to be a bridge between the church and the marketplace. We are also available to help them equip and encourage their marketplace members to live out their callings in their workplaces. Parachurch ministries such as ours exist because there is a niche or a need in the kingdom that, for the most part, is underserved or isn't being addressed. God creates an entity to fill such a gap. For us, it is the marketplace.

Over the past forty years, I have seen how the emphasis on and the understanding of marketplace ministry has increased. This has particularly been the case over the past six to eight years. The Pastors' Council, therefore, fills an important need for Needle's Eye. We've also seen that this council fills a need that pastors have. They meet frequently with those of their own denomination, but do not often meet with pastors of other denominations. When the Pastors' Council gets together, one thing I hear regularly is how thankful they are to have an entity such as Needle's Eye that creates opportunities for them to mix and mingle. Their theological perspectives and rituals may be different, but when it comes to the major points of Christianity, they universally agree. Having a forum where they can come together, associate, and get to know one another helps unify and build the body of Christ.

The last example of the foundational truth of having a kingdom mindset took place in the fall of 2016. This involved a group from Austin, Texas called We Believe. They had been conducting citywide revival-type outreaches in various metropolitan areas. The group would partner with churches in a community in an effort to raise interest in Christianity among nonbelievers. The objective over a six-week period was to attract nonbelievers to the churches on Sundays to hear talks on critical and difficult topics that nonbelievers would find of interest. Examples included, "If God exists, why do bad things happen?" and, "Is Jesus the only way to eternal life?"

We Believe produced an outreach program in Richmond called Explore God, and churches all over the Metropolitan Richmond Region were involved. Six different topics were addressed simultaneously in every pulpit during six consecutive Sundays.

Since Needle's Eye does not have a Sunday service, we adapted the topics used by the churches for seekers in the business and professional community. Over the six-week time period, we held our meetings in a bar every Tuesday night. The location we selected may appear odd, but we thought nonbelievers would find it less intimidating to attend a meeting in a bar than in a church. More than 100 Christian churches and organizations participated, and so it should not be surprising that the Explore God effort had a significant impact in our community.

God Cares about the Community in Which We Live and So Should We

Sometimes those of us in ministry become so focused on our primary constituency that, if something does not directly affect us, we may not recognize what is going on around us. Yet God wants us to care about the entire community in which we live. I believe this is another foundational truth on which a ministry should be built.

After Needle's Eye had been underway about three years, I realized my course selection in seminary in a particular area of study had been insufficient. I knew I would be taking the gospel to business people, but it did not occur to me that many of the people to whom I would be ministering would also be dealing with serious life problems. They would want or need counseling. By 1980, I was spending about half of my time in personal counseling, yet in seminary I'd only taken the basics. Consequently, I decided I needed more training in that area and enrolled with a group called

The Christian Counseling and Educational Foundation, an organization loosely affiliated with Westminster Theological Seminary
near Philadelphia.

As my counseling load continued to increase, from a scriptural perspective we began to train businessmen and women
to counsel their peers in life's difficulties. In 1981, Needle's Eye
brought a board member of The National Association of Nouthetic
Counselors (NANC) to Richmond for a weekend conference. The
purpose of the event was to provide initial training, encouragement, and motivation for attendees. We wanted them to consider
becoming more involved in a counseling ministry and to provide
an umbrella entity for such counseling—The Christian Counseling and Training Center (CCTC). To this day, CCTC fills a large
and critical need in our community. It trains counselors to help
others cope with life's problems through the application of biblical
principles.

As mentioned earlier, the homeless population was growing
rapidly in Richmond in the early eighties. It was obvious that our
constituency had been blessed and gifted by God to be business
owners, lawyers, physicians, marketing executives, and so forth.
Not only were many in a position to help financially, but more than
a few could also offer services desperately needed by the poor. I
simply could not shake this thought and eventually sent out mail-
ers asking for help.

The response was amazing! You even might say that it was
overwhelming. We began receiving money—a lot of it! Not only
did our constituency give money, but many also volunteered their
services. It wasn't long before we had a bank of volunteers along
with a good deal of money coming in regularly. We called the result
of the initial effort The CrossOver Ministry (a double entendre:
crossing over cultural lines with the cross over all). For a time we
attempted to tackle as many different hardships and difficulties as
possible. Eventually, however, God led us to focus specifically on
the medical needs of the poor. As you know, The CrossOver Ministry became The CrossOver Healthcare Ministry, now the largest
nonprofit health clinic serving the underprivileged in Virginia.

It seems apparent to me that one of the foundational truths on which to build a ministry is to be sensitive to meeting the needs of the community in which you live. Our community had an obvious need and so, by God's grace and direction, we created an entity that was not exactly in the sweet spot of our mission. However, the doctors, lawyers, and professional people who could support and provide for those needs were, and it worked out as God intended. The Great Commission begins with the words, "Go, and make disciples of all nations . . . teaching them to obey everything I commanded you . . ." (Matt 28:19). These Christian professionals were given the incredible opportunity of living out Matthew 25:31–46 by using the talents and gifts God has given them to care for those in need, specifically in need of their gifts. That is discipleship at its best!

God led us to start CrossOver in order to give our constituents an opportunity for him to use them in ways that would help them grow in their faith and discipleship. This growth happened as they experienced God using them to bless others! Their lives were impacted and changed as they lived the reality of Matthew 25:31–46.

Let's look at another example. In 1991, there was a significant downturn in construction and related industries. It was a difficult time. Companies were going out of business regularly. So we created what we called "Needle's Eye 911," the "911" portion emphasizing the sense of urgency and emergency. Our goal was to serve the needs of the community by providing help through knowledgeable volunteers (again using our base) to those having difficulty and in danger of going out of business.

We sent out a mailing to solicit this help and were able to create a bank of more than sixty volunteers. These volunteers included lawyers, accountants, tax consultants, and business owners, as well as technical and marketing specialists. About a dozen well-rounded, committed, and competent individuals were designated as team leaders. Some were business owners, attorneys, consultants, or executives of large companies. The common denominator was that all were believers.

News of this ministry spread mainly by word of mouth. When business owners learned Needle's Eye had a ministry that could help them stay in business, they would call our office, give us a synopsis of their business, and an overview of the situation they faced. We in turn would pick a team leader who would go to and assess the business. Then the team leader would call the office and report what was needed, such as a tax accountant, a lawyer, marketing person, or whomever. We would put a team together around the leader, and the team would then begin to work with the business owner.

People knew when they called Needle's Eye 911 they would be accessing a wealth of expertise and experience, and they also knew we were a faith-centered organization that could provide spiritual counseling. When we went into an office, we would deal with the business issues they faced, and we would leave them a packet and encourage them to look through it. The packet explained why we do what we do. There was no pressure for them to do anything, but it did present them with an opportunity to grow in their understanding of God and accept Christ if they had not done so already.

This went on for two and a half to three years, and during that time we worked with about seventy businesses. Some businesses were saved. Others did not make it. If determined that they must go out of business, they were advised how to proceed the right way. Most importantly, we were able to have a significant spiritual impact on quite a number of people.

During that period, not only were companies going out of business, but people were losing their jobs. To meet that need, we began our Career Transition Ministry, which we initially called The Unemployed Ministry.

I went to two individuals and asked if they could devote some time to this by stewarding a couple of small groups of unemployed peers. One had been the president of a company, but through a corporate acquisition he had lost his job. The other was a professional counselor who oversaw a group of counselors at several locations. This effort continued three to four years and eventually waned. It resurfaced in 2001, however, and in 2008 it grew so large that it threatened to overwhelm us. Fortunately, by that time we had enough volunteers to handle the load.

In June 2008, we had about twenty-five small groups. One of them was specifically for unemployed people. By October of that year, fifty people were on the rolls of our unemployed ministry. Our small group coordinator came to me and said we needed to meet the needs of this rapidly growing group. We changed her job description and duties to enable her to devote about fifty percent of her time to work with the unemployed.

By February 2009, there were 140 on our unemployed rolls, and the number was growing. We had a retired Navy Captain available, the retired company president from 1991 still involved, and leading the charge was a retired Human Resources Director from a Fortune 500 company. There were also several others involved with appropriate business backgrounds.

Between 2009 and 2012, the Career Transition Ministry helped about 600 people. In addition, our full-time small group coordinator trained a number of local churches and community-wide groups to establish their own ministries to the unemployed. By God's grace, the needs of many within our community were met. Because of these programs, people within the Needle's Eye community became the arms and hands of Christ. This provided encouragement, support, and jobs to the unemployed, and some even came to Christ through this experience.

One more example comes to mind. It involves a group in Richmond called CommonGood RVA. It is made up primarily of young business and professional men and women who are concerned about how work can affect the common good of the community. The organization had its first conference in 2014, and Needle's Eye was one of the sponsors. Several well-known speakers were brought in and presented messages to about 200 people. These messages were based upon biblical truths that can affect the common good of a community.

Amy Sherman was one of the speakers. Her book, which I would highly recommend to anyone, is called *Kingdom Calling: Vocational Stewardship for the Common Good.* The concept she drives home in this book is one in which we have always believed and to which we have subscribed. The principle is that God makes us who we are and gives us gifts, abilities, and interests for his purposes. He wants to use us, while living our lives in our communities, for the common good. The basis of this is Proverbs 11:10 (NIV):

> When the righteous prosper, the city rejoices; when the
> wicked perish, there are shouts of joy.

The righteous are people who follow God, believers who live in a way that reflects their relationship with him. The text says that when they prosper, the city rejoices. The word "prosper" in this context primarily means "prosper financially," which begs the question, "Why would that be true?"

This passage comes from the Old Testament and was written at a time when people realized that when people prospered, the gifts they received were from God and were meant for more than just those who directly received them. If they were living their faith, the city should rejoice because they would use what they received to care for others. The CommonGood RVA Conference began to sow this seed that we, as believers, have a responsibility to others and to the community in which we live.

Here is my final example of the foundational truth that God cares about the community in which we live, and so should we. Of the fifty-six small groups under the Needle's Eye umbrella, twelve are made up of presidents of companies. One, our Executive Study and Dialogue group, is slightly different in that its members represent large organizations, some of which are Fortune 500 corporations. As a result, the members of all of these groups have the ability to influence a large number of people.

Following the CommonGood RVA Conference, I asked two guests to address our Executive Study and Dialogue group. One was a pastor of an inner-city church, and the other was the executive director of a nonprofit from the inner city. They talked about what was happening in their part of town. Over the course of the discussion, the one who headed the nonprofit made a point of saying that among other issues, people in his community were having a hard time getting loans. He was talking about small loans, which most banks are not very interested in making, especially to residents of inner-city neighborhoods.

Months later, I learned that one of the men at the meeting, a bank president, had gone to that part of town, talked with the leaders of the nonprofit, and worked out an arrangement enabling small loans to be made with his bank. Caring for the community is one of God's critical principles, and from the standpoint of Needle's Eye, pursuing that principle allows us to demonstrate to our constituency what God is able to accomplish through them!

God's Ways are Different from Man's Ways

This fundamental truth needs to be taken into account not only when establishing a ministry, but also in one's life as a believer in Jesus Christ. You will probably recall the discussion in a previous chapter about open air preaching which, as you know, was one of the most difficult things I have had to address. I had a hard time getting to "yes," and a hard time actually doing it the first day. In a worldly sense, I viewed it as perhaps the least attractive way to reach business and professional men and women because it called to mind the days of street preachers on soapboxes ranting away at passersby. However, God's ways are not man's ways, and he was very specific that outdoor preaching was what he wanted us to do. I finally complied and our board did so about a year later. As a result, we reached thousands of people over five years, with a number of them coming to Christ. Actually, in a recent conversation a good friend reminded me that Jesus, in fact, did a good bit of it himself.

Another example has to do with the Needle's Eye's Board of Directors working on the basis of unanimity and realizing that successful business people make up our board.

At the end of 2013, I was in my mid-sixties. As you know, the world says that's when a person ought to retire, and the leadership of companies typically transitions from older to younger executives. Such transitions have likely been planned for quite some time. As a result, Needle's Eye had developed a strategic plan that outlined a number of initiatives, including that my successor would be recruited, and I would retire at a predetermined time. Neither Laura nor I ever felt God's peace about this, but were initially just listening to and respecting my board.

Needle's Eye had good people on the board, people committed to Christ, with good worldly reasons for moving us along that track. However, one important element was not in accord. God had not released me yet as the executive director. My passion for what I was doing was still at 100 percent, and my health was good both mentally and physically.

Nevertheless, we began to make plans for a transition. My colleague who had taken our small groups and the Career Transition Ministry to high levels was to become the director of all ministry outreach other than what I was doing personally. I would be freed to concentrate on ministry, and we would establish a process that would begin to find my replacement. We moved in this direction for several months, and then my colleague was due to go out on sabbatical.

One Saturday morning in June 2015, I sat quietly on my deck, having my quiet-time reading in 1 Timothy 6. During that devotional, God made it clear he had not released me from being Executive Director of Needle's Eye, regardless of how the world did things. Later, I shared this with the board. As of this writing, I am focused on certain ministries, and there is no retirement deadline looming. At some point, I will give up my position as Executive Director and become an emeritus something or other, but this will be as and when God leads. His ways are different from man's ways and thankfully he has blessed us with board members who love him to such an extent that they desire to follow him, even as he redirects a wise, worldly decision. Interestingly, that fall my colleague's husband unexpectedly accepted a job just outside Dallas, and they moved to Texas.

Other examples of God's ways often being different include our board criteria and our funding philosophy. Concerning the latter, we have always maintained that we will not use any heavy-handed or emotional approach, nor will we ever overstate our case. We believe God has called us to do what we do, and if we are faithful in fulfilling that calling, he is more than faithful to meet our needs.

We do, of course, make our needs known, and if we have a special project that requires funding, we will call potential donors and ask if they are open to praying about helping at a given level. Over the forty years of Needle's Eye, this philosophy has served us well. You will recall, for example, how our rainy day fund sustained us during the Great Recession. God knew what we would need long before we did.

When we are not in an economic downturn and have decided to add projects and/or people, it has always been amazing how money has come *when it was needed*. At the end of such a year, for example, the revenue would be higher, but the percentage gap between income and expenditures would be about the same. This is not to say we never have to watch expenses or occasionally make cuts so that we do not spend more than we take in. The result has always been that our needs are met—though not often with a great deal of excess, or for that matter, any at all.

The final example I want to share is that of our board membership criteria (see Addendum). The fact that we make decisions based on unanimity, as well as what I am about to explain, sets us apart from most groups. We have four criteria for board members. First, we want committed believers who are part of the business and professional community. They need to see the need for this kind of ministry and to buy into our mission. Second, we want them to be leaders in their local churches because we believe in the church. We are a parachurch ministry that fills a niche and wants to be seen as supporting, not competing with, the churches. We understand that the church is the basic entity God uses to take the gospel to the world and to grow people of faith. Third, we want board members who are actively involved in Needle's Eye. Fourth, and often the most difficult one to meet, we want someone who has been touched by the Lord through some facet of Needle's Eye.

This may have happened through our luncheons, our small groups, or our galas. However this came to be, some facet of Needle's Eye needs to have touched them and made a difference in their lives. This creates buy-in because such a person will thoroughly understand the mission once he or she has been directly affected by it.

These four points are not easily met, especially the fourth, but to my mind they are foundational and will never change. Because the fourth point is especially difficult to meet, we have begun cultivating people in the community who could become good board members, but who are not yet involved with Needle's Eye. We view this as a process of educating them about the ministry by involving them. If and when the time comes that it might make sense for them to come on the board, the four criteria will have been met.

One additional criterion, which is not written down but has been operative for us since 1977, is that we do not look for people to sit on our board simply because they have deep pockets. There are some on our board with significant resources. Through the years there have been times we could have attracted others who had the ability to generously fund Needle's Eye, and perhaps they could have recruited other wealthy donors who could generate significant financial support. However, because they did not meet the four criteria, we did not consider approaching them. We believe that when an organization primarily recruits board members based upon their ability to give, the leaders of that organization step over the line into the ways of the world. They are running the risk of trusting man instead of God. An important reason I believe we have been around for forty years is that we have tried to the best of our imperfect ability to do what we do based on his principles and how he has led us. Because of this belief, it has become clear to us that God's ways are not always man's ways.

CHAPTER SEVEN

Effective Outreach Opportunities, Part One

IN CHAPTERS 5 AND 6, we discussed personal spiritual disciplines and foundational truths. I believe these principles have been critical components as God has led and guided us the past forty years. Our staff, the Board of Directors, and others took those principles to heart, and thereby they became effective channels for the Lord, thus facilitating the goal of taking the gospel to the Richmond business and professional community. By his mercy, grace, and guidance, a solid foundation was laid for the outreach opportunities we will now consider.

Marketplace Ministry by Marketplace People Is God's Plan

As has been discussed, none of Jesus' disciples were members of the professional clergy of his day. They were ordinary people, fishermen, tax collectors, and the like. Yet Jesus called upon them to help him change the world. Our ministry follows the same logic in that in the vast majority of instances we have business and professional men and women, those who live and work in Richmond, as speakers at our luncheons and events. This has always been a tenet of Needle's Eye and is perhaps even more important and effective today than in the past. Moreover, we have found that impact and attendance are greater when a ministry event is held during the week in a hotel ballroom, conference facility, or other public venue, rather than in a church.

In 1978, we began having monthly luncheon meetings at locations in different sectors of the business community. Luncheon meetings continue to be held today. We believe the key to success was having local business and professional men and women as speakers, many of whom were well known in our community, and all of whom were believers who had committed their lives to Jesus Christ. They were willing to give their faith stories and speak about their faith. Their colleagues, friends, and peers turned out to give them support and to hear what they had to say.

Luncheons became important evangelistic opportunities. We kept them to an hour or less. Speakers would have twenty minutes to share their faith story, and I would take a few minutes to close the meetings, giving attendees an opportunity to make a commitment to Christ. I did this in a number of different ways. One was a silent prayer, and another in the early years was to ask people to raise a hand, as their heads were bowed and their eyes were closed. We do not do either today. Some years ago we began giving each person a card that could be used to indicate whether they had a desire to talk about their faith, to make a commitment to Christ, or to make a recommitment. It is perhaps an understatement to say that the number of individuals who have come to faith as a result of Needle's Eye luncheons is significant.

Citywide galas, which began in 1986, also came about as a result of our belief in marketplace ministry by marketplace people. We have offered twelve of these large events over the years and have featured a total of ten speakers, as two speakers were invited back for encore appearances.

Our first speaker was Truett Cathy, the founder of the Chick-fil-A restaurant chain. In 1986, Mr. Cathy was already well known as a Christian and as a businessman. Invitations were sent to all our constituents encouraging them to bring guests, particularly guests who were not known to be believers. We purposely held the event at an upscale venue, The Commonwealth Club, where we knew that top executives would feel at home.

That first gala drew just under 200 people from across the business spectrum, including an impressive percentage of senior executives. It was heartening to see many new faces, a significant percentage of whom subsequently became constituents of Needle's Eye and later board members. In fact, three members of our 2012 Board of Directors had come to faith as a result of one of those galas.

We continued having galas featuring nationally known members of the business world, or well-known athletes or coaches. Most importantly, all were Christian believers, and the number of people attending increased each year. In 2016, Tony Bennett, the highly successful coach of the University of Virginia basketball team, was our speaker. He spoke to a crowd of more than 400 at our gala held in The Jefferson Hotel.

In 1989, it seemed that God was showing us that we needed to provide ongoing growth opportunities for our constituents. Luncheons and galas were providing opportunities for people to connect with the Lord, but the question that kept surfacing was, "What can we do to help those new believers grow in the Lord now that they have asked him into their lives?"

At that time, there were four men, two of whom had come to us through the luncheons. I invited them to attend a six-week small group Bible study, explaining that they would have the opportunity to opt out after six weeks, or the option to continue. All four chose to continue.

The group was held early in the morning at our office, in the basement conference room we had at the time. We would take turns bringing donuts, and I led them through a basic Bible study. We also talked about our lives, and as time passed, we began to do so to an extent that went deeper than a superficial level. I used icebreakers to get personal discussions started, icebreakers such as, "Up to age eighteen, who was the most significant person in your life?" Or "Up to age twelve, what is your most significant memory?" To put others at ease, I would always answer first, and of course, we agreed that whatever was said in the room would stay in the room. Consequently, we began to open up about ourselves, and a bond of trust grew between us.

Six weeks is not a long time, but it was a moving time for each of us. As a result, at the end of the six weeks, all of us wanted the group to continue, even though initially a couple of the guys had hesitated to commit even to six weeks.

This group began meeting about six months before I attended Lausanne II, the Second International Congress on World Evangelization. The Lausanne Movement, which was created by Billy Graham and other notable Christians in 1974, was a global effort to mobilize evangelical leaders to collaborate to achieve world evangelization by the year 2000. Lausanne II was held in 1989, fifteen years later, in Manila. About thirty–five hundred Christian ministers and leaders came. The conference lasted two weeks, and there were a number of speakers. Classes also took place on a number of study tracks, and I chose small groups. The teacher of this track was an Australian named John Mallison, who was well known in the Australian-British community. He had written a couple of books on the subject, was very knowledgeable, and a terrific teacher. I returned home feeling God was leading in this. We quickly determined to add a small group outreach component to the ministry outreaches of Needle's Eye.

I next recruited five or six men and a couple of women and did some training to prepare them to become small group leaders. Several in the original small group had spoken at a luncheon series, which featured the small group concept. At the end of that series of luncheons we gave attendees the opportunity to join newly forming small groups. Those interested filled out a form that asked such questions as what time of day and part of town would work best for them. About forty people responded, enough for half a dozen or so small groups, which meant that everyone who had trained would have a group to lead. I eventually turned over the group I'd been leading to one of the members, making seven ongoing groups, all led by volunteers.

A new ministry was underway! Today, in 2017, we have a small group coordinator who trains group leaders and helps start new groups. We have nearly sixty small groups. For the most part, the groups are segregated by gender, although we do have a couple of co-ed groups. At this time, there is one career transition group, and there are twelve Christian Presidents Groups (CPGs).

CPGs came about in 1995 because several members of existing groups came to me and said they would like to be in a group with others who faced the same sort of situations they did as business owners and company presidents. We searched our rolls and culled thirty whom we knew well and matched that profile. We also drew information from YPO (the Young Presidents' Organization, a global network of young chief executives), as well as other sources. We invited those owners and presidents to attend a meeting at a country club. We explained what we had in mind and asked if they would like to be in such a group. Enough said yes that we were able to start three groups.

When a new CPG starts up, I typically will act as the facilitator for three or four months. After that, a group member will take over and lead for a couple of years before rotating the leadership duties to another member. Again, marketplace ministry done by marketplace people.

In 2002, a good friend and my personal dentist, who would bring his staff to our luncheons virtually every month, called me and said he had a concern he wanted to discuss. He had been involved with Needle's Eye for more than twenty years and had spoken for us on several occasions. When we met, he had recently sold his practice and was going to retire in a few months. He was worried about what he was going to do, but he said he felt God had something in mind for him. We talked, and it became evident he felt compassion for his contemporaries who were struggling with the same concerns that he had in that stage of life, as well as for those who didn't know the Lord.

This man had a heart for Christ and was a leader who could motivate others, so I encouraged him to follow that passion. He, along with two others, began what we now call the Second Half Ministry, made up of men who are retired or close to retirement.

They began meeting every two weeks in his church. They have a sharing time and usually a guest speaker. Then they break into small groups, share personally, and have a lesson for about forty-five minutes.

The Second Half Ministry now has four locations and more than 175 men are involved. They care for one another, grow together in faith, and some have come to faith. They also care for the community through working with a disabled member, mentoring younger businessmen, and so forth, as God leads them. Marketplace ministry by marketplace people is working in their group, just as God intended.

Meet the Felt Needs of Your Target Audience

The Needle's Eye target audience has always been business and professional men and women with a focus on the white-collar community. That's the one I grew up in and the community from which I came as a businessman. You will remember that my very wise seminary advisor once said, "Buddy, wouldn't it be like God to use your past for his future?"

As with every market segment, this group has needs, and perhaps the most profound is for counseling. This need exists regardless of how much money a person earns. In some cases, difficulties may surface, and the need for counseling may result, because money has become more important than what ought to be of most value to an individual. As you will recall from an earlier discussion, in the third and fourth years of Needle's Eye, I was spending more time counseling than I had anticipated, so I decided to take some training at the Christian Counseling and Educational Foundation near Philadelphia. This led to the start of a new ministry we called the Christian Counseling Center, which later became known as the Christian Counseling and Training Center.

At the time, I was counseling six to eight cases a week and was doing some training as well. We held a weekend seminar, which provided more training, and within a year we had eight counselors and several courses being taught.

By 1984, we had ten lead counselors and another fifteen to twenty in training. We were also handling fifteen to twenty cases a week. Peers were meeting the counseling needs of those in the business and professional community, peers who loved Christ and were willing to undergo training. In other words, marketplace people were meeting the felt needs of people in the marketplace.

God has given each of us gifts and has a purpose for us that involves using those gifts to help others. The extent of the gifts our particular constituency has received is vast, and this became even more apparent to me as my contacts in the business and professional community grew over time. You will recall from a discussion in chapter 6 that I became convicted that our constituency could help mitigate some of the needs I saw around me, such as homelessness and poverty. We put together a board and mounted an effort to encourage and lead those whom God had blessed with gifts, abilities, and resources so they might effectively use them to bless those in need.

This resulted in what became an enormously successful outreach, the CrossOver Ministry, now the largest such healthcare ministry in Virginia. It happened due to the commitment of a core of people (CrossOver's initial board and bank of volunteers) to serve our community. It also came about as a result of efforts to meet the needs of our target audience. An important need each one of us has is to allow God to use what we have been given to help and benefit others. The community benefited, and many in our target audience benefited as well because they grew in faith and discipleship as a result of this outreach.

You will also recall from the previous chapter the outreach effort we mounted in 1991 to meet the needs of our target audience when the construction industry took a dramatic downturn. Needle's Eye 911 was created to help mitigate the effects of that recession. We saw this as part of the very fabric of our ministry.

These struggling business owners and the resulting unemployed business people became our "least of these." This program continued for close to three years, during which time we worked with approximately seventy businesses.

The majority of those businesses stayed afloat. Others did not make it, but at least those that went under did so in the right way. Most importantly, we were able to have a significant spiritual impact on a large number of people. Moreover, Needle's Eye 911 became the forerunner of our Career Transition Ministry, which reached its peak during the Great Recession, but also continues to play an important role in people's lives today.

Another example of meeting the needs of our target audience is a seminar we brought to Richmond in 1991 called "Dad the Family Shepherd." This was a ministry created by a former NFL linebacker to help teach and encourage men to be good fathers. I knew from personal experience that our target audience had this need. This was not only evident from my early years as a dad, but as a result of much of the personal counseling I'd been doing.

Many who grew up in my generation, the Boomer generation, had fathers who may have been present in the home, but were not very attentive. They were members of the Greatest Generation, men who lived through the Great Depression, fought a war, and learned important life lessons as a result. Nevertheless, those horrific events were not the best tools needed when it came to learning how to be a good husband and father.

This weekend-long conference was held in a local church. More than 400 men representing eighty-nine churches attended. Approximately fifty follow-up groups formed as a result, each of which continued meeting weekly for six to twelve weeks. A one-time outreach to meet the felt needs of our target audience, it literally changed for the better many of the homes represented. It was so powerful that in the first night of the conference forty men prayed to receive Christ! To this day, I still hear about that seminar.

When considering our target audience, it goes without saying that from the beginning we have always been concerned with the spiritual and practical needs of marketplace men and women.

Early on, I was leading seminars and teaching in churches, locally and beyond, on calling, the theology of work, and the practical implications of each.

Building on those early years, we brought Doug Sherman and Bill Hendricks to Richmond in November 1992 to conduct a conference on *Your Work Matters to God*. There were more than 400 men and women in attendance at the Richmond Center for this two-day offering. Co-chaired by two of our board members, the president and executive vice president of a local technology company, this event was outstanding. Many returned to their workplaces enlightened and empowered to see and do their work as God had intended.

A very significant, meaningful, and effective outreach for over twenty years was our specific outreach to women in the workplace. Since Needle's Eye's inception, we have always been a ministry "to the men and women of Richmond's business and professional community." In fact, the first person to come to faith through Needle's Eye was a female paralegal.

During the early years, the landscape of the marketplace shifted, and the overall culture changed. Women in the workplace had specific needs. Their lives were and still are overly full. Like men, they benefit from being in groups with others like themselves where they can fellowship and minister to one another.

In the early 1990s, one of our board members, a female attorney named Lake Monhollon, volunteered to purposefully lead a few women's small groups and to meet with women one-on-one in a ministry context. She became our first Director of Women's Ministry in 1994. However, her husband subsequently took a teaching position at Hardin-Simmons University in Texas, which caused them to leave Richmond. Concurrently, Caren Crosby Fields was also a board member and became our chairwoman in August 1994. For years she had been a highly successful Sales Director for Mary Kay Cosmetics, consistently winning pink Cadillacs and other types of vehicles while directing a team of some 100 sales consultants. Caren succeeded Lake and became our first Director of Women's Ministry as a part-time staff member.

Remember that nightclub hostess in chapter 2? The one whose boss regularly brought her to our monthly luncheons? Remember how she subsequently came to faith and became involved in a Christian ministry? That nightclub hostess was Caren.

In 2002, Caren came to me and said that due to changes in her personal life, she felt the Lord was leading her to resign. After being single for twenty years, Caren was now a newlywed, and a grandmother, and her Mary Kay business was demanding more of her time.

An interesting conversation followed as she shared, "Buddy, I think I know who my replacement will be."

I responded, "Who?"

She said, "Jennifer Parham."

My immediate response was, "Caren, you have lost your mind!"

Jennifer Parham was a bright, hardworking, and capable young attorney at one of the larger law firms in Richmond. I had known her for years, as she had grown up in the church where my family and I had been members since 1980. After months of discussion and prayer, in 2002, Jennifer accepted our offer to become our next Director of Women's Ministry. Later, she became our first full-time director and built on the work of Lake and Caren, taking our Women's Ministry to a different level. Jennifer resigned in 2014 to return to the practice of law.

Over the years, the Lord has used Needle's Eye's Women's Ministry in wonderful ways. Offerings available to the marketplace women of Richmond have included small group meetings, Bible studies, retreats, special speaker events, and opportunities for one-on-one counseling and discipleship.

Meeting the felt needs of our constituency and community has taken on several different forms over our forty years. Always driving it, however, has been our desire to meet the most pressing and real need: that everyone has to meet and have a personal relationship with the One who made each and every one us.

CHAPTER EIGHT

Effective Outreach Opportunities, Part Two

IN CHAPTER 7, WE looked at two of our Twelve Truths in light of ministry outreaches and their format. The fact that God uses marketplace people for ministry purposes should not take us by surprise. Remember the disciples? There wasn't a Pharisee or priest among them!

Meeting felt needs is a major principle throughout Scripture. Matthew 25:31–46 and Luke 8:38–39 are two of many examples.

In this chapter we will address two other truths that are outreach oriented: "Go where the lost are," and "Methods change but the message never does." In several of the outreaches addressed, we will see marketplace people on the delivery end of ministry going where the lost are. We may also see some unusual outreaches that begin to prick the conscience relative to our deepest need.

Go Where the People are Who Don't Know the Lord

Since we began, our mission has been to take the gospel of Jesus Christ, and all the ethics implied therein, to Richmond's business and professional communities, specifically to men and women who do not know him. He is the ultimate change agent, the One who changes lives and empowers people to live differently. Once that happens, the business community can become a different place. To accomplish this means going where the lost are. I'd like to share four of the many ways we have done so.

We have already discussed the Needle's Eye luncheons. We began these early on because it was clear that most nonbelievers would not be found in church on Sunday mornings. They are often more likely to be on the tee or sleeping in. However, they will be found at work Monday through Friday, eight to five. This is why we have primarily used the lunch hour and why we held the luncheons in the various business districts of our metropolitan area. During the course of a month, we would hold one in the downtown financial district, another in a large suburban office development in the Far West End, another on the other side of the James River in South Richmond, and in Mechanicsville in the East End near the airport. We also found that speakers who are peers, perhaps even colleagues, are effective at presenting nonbelievers with the message of God's love and grace and his ability to change their lives.

Over the years, we have held more than 750 luncheons with more than 300 speakers. The majority of our speakers have been local, and many were well known to a large number of our business and professional community.

At one time, we actually held five luncheons a month, each in a different part of town. During that period, we would have two speakers. One would speak at three luncheons, and the other at two. When four luncheons were held during a month, the same speaker would address each of them, which of course was a significant commitment for a businessperson during the work week.

As has been discussed, another way we took the gospel where the lost would be found was through outdoor preaching. That effort, which took place on the Capitol grounds, went on for five years and required a government permit. As you know, we felt uncomfortable about doing this at first, but it became obvious to all that it was what God wanted us to do.

After the first year, we had guest pastors preach the first four days of the week. One, a well-known Richmond pastor who had a TV ministry and spoke to thousands every Sunday, told me he had never preached outdoors and was nervous about doing so. In spite of his trepidation, he did a marvelous job.

Part of the regimen of this outreach was that each pastor was asked to have leaders from his church, deacons, elders, or vestrymen, stand on street corners within a five-block area of the Capitol during the lunch hour exactly one week before he was to preach. Their responsibility was to pass out fliers promoting the upcoming event.

For the most part, the people handing out fliers also worked downtown. Often, they would put fliers into the hands of their colleagues who were on their way to lunch. Some of them told me this was one of the hardest things they'd ever had to do as a Christian. For these men and women, this is a wonderful example of God's truth that "obedience is critical, but doesn't always equate with comfort."[1] However, we were determined to go where the lost could be found, and we did so in a way we knew would be different and not always easy.

Those outdoor events would begin each day at 12:10 and would conclude within forty minutes. We used a borrowed sound system that was second to none. In fact, it was so powerful that a clerk from a federal court two blocks away called the governor's office and asked them to request that the volume be turned down because they were having trouble concentrating on the court proceedings.

We employed other strategies to gain and retain a crowd. For example, we had music at the beginning of each service to gather a crowd. The guest preacher would deliver a twenty-minute message in two ten-minute segments. After the first ten minutes, a businessperson would come to the microphone to give a short personal testimony about how Christ had changed his or her life. The preacher would then return to the microphone for another ten minutes. Breaking things up this way helped keep the crowd's attention.

The pastors were asked to have six to ten counselors present on the grounds when it was each one's turn to preach. When he

1. See the "12 Truths" sheet in the Addendum.

or she finished preaching, I would take a few minutes to close. I'd tell the audience that if they had heard something that raised their interest spiritually, there were people in the audience who would be available to talk with them and, perhaps, pray with them. Then I would ask the individuals from the pastor's church to raise their hands so that everyone would know who they were. Inevitably, some in the audience would go to them. The important point I'm hoping to make here is that we adapted to the venue we had selected because it was where the lost could be found.

Here is another example. You will remember I mentioned that in 2001, I read an article in the newspaper about a program in the D.C./Northern Virginia area called Theology on Tap, the Roman Catholic ministry to young Catholics that met in a bar. I recall thinking this was a fantastic idea and was something Jesus himself would have done since the lost are not going to be found in a church. When my board chairman and I went to Georgetown to check it out, we saw about 250 people there, mostly young, and the vast majority of them standing. We entered, approached the bar, and were immediately embarrassed by two young women who got up and gave us their seats. Then a priest spoke, followed by someone who was not a priest and talked about a life issue, tying it to the church. Then there were about thirty minutes for questions and answers.

After a second visit by a majority of our board, we formed a committee and put together the program. As you know, we called it Spiritual Shots. It continued through 2015, taking place in a bar once a month for eight to nine months each year. Over time these sessions evolved to the point that such difficult questions as "If God is good, why is there so much difficulty in the world?," "Why are babies born deformed?" and, "Is Jesus really the only way to the Father?" were asked and addressed.

To gather and entertain the crowd, we had live music, and we provided free pizza. Attendees had to buy their own beer, wine, or soft drinks. The featured speaker was usually a pastor who would come and spend fifteen minutes speaking on a topic such as those listed above, and then a Q-&-A session would follow. You can be assured that there was much lively but mutually respectful inter-action with atheists and other nonbelievers present. Suffice it to say, Spiritual Shots is another positive and productive example of going where the lost could be found.

My final example of going where the lost could be found be-gan in September 1986. Earlier that year, we let people know at our luncheons that we were going to hold a weekly Bible study at a restaurant on Friday mornings. We selected a place where busi-ness people would feel comfortable. A hot breakfast was available and the service was good. Perhaps our original location was too comfortable because it was a hotel restaurant/nightclub, still smell-ing of cigarettes and beer from the previous night. Our location changed several times but usually to a restaurant or hotel where the group's presence was obvious to others. Occasionally regulars brought guests who sometimes were seekers. By God's grace, some of these seekers committed their lives to Christ. Others grew in faith, and others saw their faith renewed. Over the years, about 100 from a number of backgrounds and denominations came and went. We had an average weekly attendance of about ten to twenty. A diverse, co-ed crowd, it was made up of business owners, college professors, one college president, salespeople, business executives, and IT gurus. There was a good deal of interaction with whatever text we were studying, and people got to know one another, even though it was not designed as a typical small group. This group continued meeting for more than fifteen years. Due to my grow-ing list of responsibilities, I handed the group off to three of its longstanding members a few years before it ended. They led it thoughtfully, passionately, and well. As I look back on Needle's Eye Ministries' early years, Friday Morning Bible Study was a long-running blessing where deep friendships were formed, God's word was studied, and, by his grace, lives were changed for his purposes and glory.

The Methods Will Change
But the Message Never Does

When thinking about and planning an outreach effort, it's important to keep in mind that times change, and people change with the times. As a result, we constantly try to stay relevant, and in doing so we keep in mind that our methods often must change in order to remain effective, but our message will never change! For five years, outdoor preaching on the Capitol grounds was effective. We had a theme for each week which had a gospel component to it, and each pastor had to preach on that theme. It was different. It was controversial, but it worked very well for a time.

Golf and tennis tournaments, on the other hand, were effective in the 1980s and 1990s, but we are not certain as to whether they would be as effective today. When we held them, we could depend on a well-known touring pro, one who also happened to be a Christian, to draw a significant number of participants.

Only constituents who were golfers and known believers would get an invitation to the golf tournaments. They would be told in the invitation that this was an outreach event, and we wanted them to bring a seeker. They paid for their golf as well as for the guest and spouse to come to dinner that night.

Typically, there would be twenty-two or twenty-four foursomes. The golf portion of such an event would take place for half a day, preceded by a clinic held by the pro. A shotgun start would follow, and the pro would play a par-three with every foursome. That way all the golfers would have an opportunity to personally meet the pro. That evening players and their spouses were invited to a banquet, and the pro would share his Christian testimony.

The golf venue was probably one of the most productive from the standpoint of the percentage of nonbelievers in attendance who were affected spiritually in a positive way. People came to faith. Ten such events were held with eight speakers, as we brought back one of the golf pros three times.

We also had two tennis tournaments. One featured Stan Smith, a Hall of Fame player, and the other, Gene Mayer, who won fourteen singles titles during his professional career. The format was much the same as the golf event. There was a clinic and a round robin tournament, followed by a dinner with spouses where the player shared his testimony.

Another example of times changing but the message staying the same comes from the 1980s. One of our constituents, a woman who was a marketing professional, had an idea a minute. One was that Needle's Eye should advertise by putting up billboards. The objective was what I have come to call cultural sensitization, i.e., priming people to consider the claims of Christ. She told me if I would get some billboards printed, she would be able to get the space for them donated at no cost. We had twenty boards printed. Each one had an image of a briefcase and said, "Jesus Christ is at work in Richmond. Consult him today." Our logo was at the bottom.

Most of the boards stayed up for at least several months, and a few were up much longer. They were on interstates and other high-traffic thoroughfares, and they definitely got people's attention. We did not have data to track the effectiveness, but the feedback we received indicated they did the job for which they were intended.

My final example of methods changing, but not the message, is the radio campaign discussed in chapter 5, the goal of which was also cultural sensitization. We wanted to prepare people for and entice them to come to a Needle's Eye luncheon or other event and perhaps to go to church with open ears and open hearts.

One spot had to do with work and a man losing his job. Another dealt with ethics and had to do with cheating on an expense report. One addressed marriage priorities, and there was the spot described in chapter 5 in which a man has just closed his biggest deal ever. He is on the phone sharing his excitement with his wife as he is killed in a car wreck. The issue of the possibility of eternal life is addressed here. The final spot depicted a young girl calling her dad, trying to get through to him at the office. She called repeatedly to remind him he had promised to take her to the library that evening. Because of her dad's busy schedule and questionable priorities, each time she tried she was only able to reach his voicemail. The radio spots ran periodically for over two years and, based on anecdotal evidence, they had a significant impact in our community.

At the time, the billboard and radio campaigns seemed to be right for the times. Because of the culture at that particular time, we felt God leading us to do something different. Whether it was outdoor preaching, billboards, meetings in bars, or the radio campaign, the key to whatever success we may have had was to be sensitive to what course of action God was directing us to take. In doing so, it was important to be open to whatever method would be effective, given the atmosphere of the day. Yet it was also essential to keep in mind that the message should and would never change!

As we close this chapter, we also keep in mind its predecessor. Chapters 7 and 8 are outreach-oriented and build upon the personal disciplines and foundational truth of chapters 5 and 6. Together, these Twelve Truths are not only a wonderful underpinning for a ministry to the marketplace, but also the lives of marketplace people. We will draw on them as we move into the current and future times of Needle's Eye Ministries.

CHAPTER NINE

So, Where are We Now
and Where are We Going?

IN THE FALL OF 2016, in the midst of our fortieth year, my colleague Jordon Maroon and I attended the National Faith at Work Summit in Dallas. For me this conference brought back memories of meetings with previous marketplace ministry practitioners and thinkers. Those meetings occurred in the eighties, nineties, and early 2000s in various locations around the country. They took place in Boston, facilitated by Dan Smick (Executive Director of Marketplace Ministries). Bob Buford (founder of Leadership Network) generously sponsored multiple meetings in Colorado Springs, where Fred Smith (Leadership Network) and Pete Hammond (Vice President of InterVarsity's marketplace and graduate school divisions) served as facilitators. Pete Hammond also served as facilitator in Chicago and at The Cove. Pat Morely (author of *Man in the Mirror*) facilitated in Knoxville, and there were other locations over the years.

It was good to see some old friends and colleagues at the Dallas conference. It was also good and stimulating to hear from new ones. One of those we most enjoyed and from whom we learned a great deal was Mark Greene, Executive Director of the London Institute for Contemporary Christianity. He spoke on Whole Life Discipleship (WLD), which was the theme of the Saturday morning closing segment. The message highlighted his "6 Ms for Fruitful Living on the Front Line." The 6 Ms will be a basic cog in the wheels of ministry delivery for Needle's Eye. For the remainder of our fortieth year, we considered what WLD would look like in our ministry deliverables and philosophy for that year and years to come.

6 Ms for Fruitful Living on the Frontline:

- Modeling God's Character
- Making Good Work
- Ministering Grace & Love
- Molding Culture
- Mouthpiece for Truth & Justice
- Messenger for the Gospel (Anywhere)

Needle's Eye has consistently made efforts to remain relevant. In the summer of 2017, as we began our forty-first year, board members and ministry partners were praying and planning for the next forty. That fall we had held a citywide conference on the theology of work/work-as-calling, which included a segment on the future workplace. This conference was led by the Rev. Dr. Ken Barnes, Professor of Workplace Theology and Business Ethics at Gordon-Conwell Theological Seminary. More than twenty-five churches and parachurch organizations helped promote this event. We purposefully prayed, strategized, and waited to receive input from this conference before we began to plan definitively for the coming years. We then used board and staff retreats as well as the Ken Barnes conference to prayerfully seek God's will for our future. As we did, we processed all possible outreach options through three filters: 1) Evangelism (always our heartbeat), 2) Whole Life Discipleship, and 3) Theology of work/work-as-calling. We also made very slight changes to our mission and values statements (see Addendum) in order to be more current with the marketplace as it evolved.

Evangelism and the theology of work/work-as-calling have always been the underpinnings of Needle's Eye. So now let me spend some time explaining the new, third underpinning—Whole Life Discipleship (WLD).

Discipleship, even whole life to some degree, is not new to us. However, what is new is the degree to which Mark Greene defines discipleship and his offering of a "package" of six tracks that must consistently be discussed, reflected upon, and lived. WLD is sure to be exciting for every believer, church, denomination, and movement that will embrace it, because it is discipleship as it was meant to be. It is the lifestyle the church was intended to employ, and we believe it is the magnet that will draw the culture back to the church and therefore, most importantly, to Christ.

Let me explain. The Great Commission has everything to do with commitment, transformation, and focus. Here it is (Matthew 28:19–20 NIV):

> Therefore go and make disciples of all nations, baptizing them in the name of the Father and of the Son and of the Holy Spirit, and teaching them to obey everything I have commanded you. And surely I am with you always, to the very end of the age.

Believers are to focus on going and making. We are not to remain stationary. We are to "make disciples," disciplined followers of Jesus, by ". . . teaching them to obey everything he commanded." This commission covers all aspects of our lives. It means loving God (Matt 22:27); caring for the disenfranchised (Matt 25:37–46); serving/putting others first (Matt 20:20–28); not being anxious or worrying, but trusting God (Matt 6:25–34); not living in anger or at odds with a brother (Matt 5:21–24); and loving our neighbor as ourselves (Matt 22:39). Therefore, in our relationships, attitude, and community, we are to live our lives as his disciplined followers.

We spend 60 percent of our waking hours at our work. Consequently, this is where we should be living for him. Why? Because the workplace is also where the world and its worshipers reside during the majority of their waking hours. The apostle Paul said that once we are in Christ we become new and different people (2

Cor 5:17–21). In Romans 12: 1–2, he goes on to explain how we can grow deeper in our walk with Christ. Therefore, "we take every thought," (2 Cor 10:5–6) word and deed captive for Christ—WLD!

In Romans 12:1, without actually using the phrase, Paul talks about how we actually live out whole life discipleship. He says, "Therefore, I urge you, brothers, in view of God's mercy, to offer your bodies as living sacrifices, holy and pleasing to God—this is your spiritual act of worship" (NIV). In a culture that perhaps was the most opulent and self-serving that has existed until the present day, Paul talks to the people of the Roman church about living their faith in Christ in the context of such a day. He says that they need to present their bodies as living sacrifices, holy and pleasing to God.

This means whatever I do with my body needs to be done in the context of God's truth directing me and God's spirit empowering me. This must be an ongoing process that does not end until this life is finished.

In verse 2, he continues to press the point, "Do not conform any longer to the pattern of this world, but be transformed by the renewing of your mind" (NIV).

In these two verses, Paul has encapsulated the truth of how we are to live as Christ would have us live in a culture that is the opposite of his truth. As we live out our lives day to day, the actions of our bodies are to be representative of God's truth. Transformation occurs as we allow our minds to be renewed by prayer, Scripture reading and memorization, and other spiritual disciplines. All of this is ultimately facilitated through the power of the indwelling Spirit.

We are to be transformed through the renewal of our minds, and our renewed minds control our bodies. As we reflect on Romans 12:1–2, we see that the mind and the body of a redeemed person are to change, and the Holy Spirit must bring about that change. In other words, through the power of the indwelling Spirit, we allow God to control our minds and therefore our bodies. When this happens, we reflect his holiness in every relationship, thought, deed, and every place we go, because once we are redeemed, we no longer are our own. We are his, 24/7/365—Whole Life Discipleship!

Graham Cray, in the 2018 spring edition of Scripture Union's *Encounter With God* devotional says it well: "In the overall direction of our lives and at each individual moment of choice we are supposed to yield ourselves to God. We make ourselves, with all our capacities, available to him. Each ability, each choice becomes an instrument or even a weapon in God's hands."[1]

The Current and Future Direction of Needle's Eye, Some of the Old

Where are we going? We believe the Lord has used the three principles or filters mentioned earlier, the experiences of the past forty-plus years with which he has blessed us, and the Twelve Truths to position Needle's Eye Ministries for the future. In looking ahead, let me share with you what we already have on the calendar or are seriously considering for the future.

- *Our Young Professionals (YPs) Outreach*

With a couple of starts and stops in the late nineties and early 2000s, this ministry component of Needle's Eye got its legs toward the end of 2010 through the efforts of Lisa Rattner, our first Small Group Coordinator. Over four-plus years, this incredibly talented, energetic, and tenderhearted licensed clinical social worker from Hoboken, New Jersey gathered together some 200 millennials. Some came to Christ, many deepened their walks with Christ, and all became a community of Christ for one another.

In 2015, Lisa's husband took a position with a large Texas-based company, and they moved to Dallas. In 2016, the Lord brought us Jordan Maroon, our second Small Group Coordinator. A millennial, married with children, this young man had

---

1. Graham Cray, "Do the Math," in *Encounter With God* (Valley Forge, PA: Scripture Union USA, April–June, 2018), 55.

previously served with InterVarsity for ten years as a campus minister—three at Wake Forest and seven at the University of North Carolina at Chapel Hill. During the last six years at UNC, he led InterVarsity's thrust and a team of four full-time staff members. An intelligent young man and a gifted teacher, Jordan has a heart for evangelism and discipleship. Before he came to Needle's Eye, he had trained more than 2,500 small group leaders with InterVarsity. He now not only directs our Small Group Ministry, but also the Young Professionals outreach.

In the summer of 2017, we sponsored a networking event for our YPs and PPs (Prime Professional—Gen-Xers). The purpose was to gather new young people to Needle's Eye and to provide them with a felt need benefit they would appreciate and use.

We reserved the outside deck at the oldest craft brewery in Richmond, which has a great view of our downtown skyline. This event was billed as an in-depth discussion on LinkedIn, the professional online networking tool now used by many, but which was not used by many millennials at the time. We provided a speaker on the use and benefits of LinkedIn and had a panel of business users that fielded questions. We also provided all attendees with a free professional headshot photo to use on LinkedIn, as well as the opportunity to grow their network and increase their personal marketability. A local photographer currently in one of our Christian President Groups (CPGs) graciously offered his services to about 100 attendees. During this two-hour event, we also offered free appetizers and shared some information about Needle's Eye.

This model of felt need networking opportunities and workshops will be a staple for us for at least the foreseeable future. We believe that topics such as work-life balance, career change, gifts assessment, and other issues will draw YPs and PPs regardless of their spiritual interest.

Currently, we are launching a mentoring initiative intended to benefit young men and young women. We have long desired to provide mentoring to the younger marketplace constituency of Richmond, and we are extremely enthusiastic about the method we will employ. We will be using book studies in which two older men will mentor four mentees, all six reading the same book. The women's initiative will bring together two seasoned Christian women and three younger mentees. We decided on a group approach rather than one-on-one because we believe it will initially result in a more relaxed environment in which barriers come down and bonds build more quickly. The initial book selections are *Men of Courage* by Dr. Larry Crabb, and *Women of the Word* by Jen Wilkin and Matt Chandler.

Interest in having a mentor is a prerequisite for younger participants wishing to take part in this new initiative. While there are no further obligations after the eight-week book study has been completed, we believe relationships will have been built that are likely to continue. Should they desire to continue in a deepening relationship, it will be the mentees' responsibility to request it. If the current mentor is unavailable, we will find the mentee another. We are excited about what this can do for both mentees and mentors, and for the kingdom!

For the past two years, our YP and PP outreach efforts have featured a Super Bowl party at a local sports bar. Each year we have had a private room and offered free appetizers. This year we changed locations, thereby securing a larger venue with TV screens galore, ping-pong, corn hole, and so forth. Each year we have had about 100 in attendance, many of whom we had never seen before. Opportunities like this, to reach a new and broader audience, will become a staple of our YP and PP outreaches as they continue to draw in younger marketplace people to Needle's Eye.

Finally, to create an opportunity to reach out and connect with other active groups of younger marketplace people in Richmond, we will be hosting a luncheon for the leaders of the significant millennial networks in the metropolitan area. There are seven such networking groups within that age range. This spring we will host a lunch for their leaders in order to plan networking events for millennials throughout the community in the coming year. These events will be structured in order to allow young professionals in the city to become aware of other great groups and to provide relationship and network building opportunities. Only two of the seven groups represented are faith based.

- *Some Old Strategies and Some With New Twists*

Since the mid-eighties, Needle's Eye has used large events and galas as methods to reach nonbelievers. These have proved fruitful. They have included banquets featuring well-known speakers sharing faith stories, as well as golf tournaments ending in an evening banquet with a PGA touring pro sharing his testimony. Providing these large events has provided an opportunity for many of our constituents to come together and introduce their colleagues and friends to Needle's Eye and perhaps even to the Lord. Going forward, we foresee having at least one such event per year.

Periodically throughout our history we have held seminars on personal evangelism. The purpose of these seminars is to help equip marketplace people to comfortably and effectively share their faith stories. This has always been a core component of Needle's Eye and will continue to be so. We have reviewed and updated materials to make them more conducive to the current culture. We have changed some of the methods, but we have not changed, nor will we ever change, the message. Our passion will always be to share that message and, by God's grace, to see lives changed.

For more than twenty-five years we have provided ministry, encouragement, practical skills training, and advice to the unemployed in our community through our Career Transition Ministry. We will continue to do so because we see unemployed marketplace people as our "least of these." One of our methods of supporting members of our Career Transition Group is the Career Development Workshop. This eight-week, three-hour-per-week workshop is led by a retired HR director of a Fortune 500 company. It addresses such topics as interview skills, résumé writing, improved networking, and job search skills. Over the years this workshop has proved to be extremely helpful to hundreds.

Lastly, we will be reintroducing our Peer Group luncheons. We used these luncheons in the eighties and nineties to reach nonbelievers in the marketplace of Richmond. Over the years we have held these vertical marketplace luncheons for lawyers, real estate brokers, dentists, certified public accountants, bankers, and the like. The idea is simple. For the lawyer luncheon, we asked several lawyers involved with Needle's Eye to host a luncheon (or it could be a breakfast). We wanted them to invite peers and colleagues as their guests. The idea was to have each of the hosts (usually three or four) invite ten to fifteen guests. The hosts would pay for the event, and it would be held at a restaurant or private club. Invitation letters would go out on one of their letterheads along with all their signatures. The invitation stated that the host would like for the recipient to be his or her guest to learn about an organization that has played a significant role in the host's life—Needle's Eye Ministries.

The event itself would last no more than an hour, a portion of which would be dedicated to the personal faith story of one of the hosts. Following that testimony, I would give a brief overview of the history and purpose of Needle's Eye, as well as a few current opportunities available through Needle's Eye. We would take a few questions and then close with prayer.

Following the meeting, the hosts would go over the attendance list with me to plan for further follow-up. That might be a personal visit or an invitation to a short three- or four-session Bible study on exploring personal faith.

Given the difficulties we face today with overloaded schedules and time shortages, the Peer Group luncheon offers a more comfortable venue than a citywide, general marketplace luncheon such as the ones we held in past decades. We believe a personal invitation from a friend or colleague desiring to share something that has been important to that individual can be the most inviting and compelling type of invitation.

- *The New Twists*

We will continue the Speaker's Series, which was once called the Luncheon Series and had been the centerpiece of Needle's Eye for over thirty years. As you may recall, well-known individuals in the Richmond business community would tell how they came to faith in Jesus Christ and how their faith affected their professional lives. In recent years, however, it has become increasingly difficult for many people to break away for an hour or so at lunchtime. Additionally, the culture is such that pure testimonies are no longer as compelling as they once were in motivating spiritual seekers to attend an event. After a good deal of prayer, thought, and discussion, we believe that having Christians address felt needs in the workplaces will be more meaningful to believers and more winsome to seekers.

Rather than sharing their faith stories, we will ask well-known marketplace men and women to explain how they deal with relevant workplace issues and problems through the filter of their faith in Christ. Such talks will take place at a breakfast, lunch, or an event after work. Topics will include such felt needs as dealing with criticism in the workplace, living a lifestyle of busyness, handling office conflicts, dealing with difficult workers, and how loving one's neighbor includes the workplace neighbor. We believe that addressing these practical, everyday problems will be meaningful to believers and nonbelievers alike, and will fulfill the truth of Matthew 5:16 (NIV): "In the same way, let your light shine before men, that they may see your good deeds and praise your Father in heaven."

Our Spring 2018 Speaker Series featured two well-known and deeply committed people. The former Police Chief of nearby Henrico County, Col. Douglas Middleton, addressed the topic of handling criticism at work. Considering his professional background, he had plenty of examples to share. Justin Earley, a former missionary, author, and now a lawyer in the largest firm in Richmond, spoke on dealing the crisis of busyness. We view this outreach as an example of whole-life discipleship designed to equip believers to live their faith in every aspect of their lives, particularly in the workplace.

Another opportunity that is new, but tied to an ongoing outreach, has to do with our Christian Presidents Groups (CPGs), which began at the end of 1995. We plan to put more emphasis on this effort because we see it as having great potential to affect the culture of our city. These are people who are responsible for others. Some are responsible for thousands of employees as well as numerous vendors and clients, making their ability to impact the culture absolutely incredible. Living their faith as the most important component of their lives is both winsome and biblical. It has a way of positively spilling over into the communities in which they live and work.

Typically these groups meet monthly for four hours, and we bring them together once or twice a year for a corporate meeting. Years ago, we also had retreats where we would go away for a weekend. This retreat aspect will take on a new perspective as the future unfolds. Here's why. In 2017, one of the members of the group of which I am a part of died. He had been our group facilitator for years. His name was Wilton Ford, and he was well known locally. He graduated from Manchester High School in Richmond, and he played basketball at the University of Richmond, where he is now in the Athletic Hall of Fame. He holds several records. One about which he was more than a little chagrined is the record for fouling out of the most games! This is particularly unique because he did so at a time when freshman athletes were not allowed to play on varsity teams. He therefore set and still holds the record with only three years of varsity experience!

Wilton was a good businessman and a faithful family man. When he died, it shocked and saddened many people. Out of love and with due appreciation for his life, one of Wilton's friends made a seed gift that attracted additional gifts by people who knew and loved him. The result is that Needle's Eye has been given $100,000, which now comprises the Wilton Ford Fund. The money will be used for programs about which Wilton would likely have been excited and in which he would have participated.

The first of these opportunities will be a reactivation of the CPG retreats, and we now have the ability to bring in outside speakers. The goal will be to help equip CPG men and women to live more effectively as whole-life disciples, thereby making more of a positive impact on the workplaces and communities in which God has placed them. We hope to see the first of many such opportunities occur soon.

- *New Outreaches Within Effective, Existing Ministries*

Needle's Eye has been significantly involved in small group ministry since 1989. We currently have close to sixty groups with over eighty qualified and trained leaders.

A new small group outreach has been launched as a follow up to the event held last fall that featured the Rev. Dr. Ken Barnes. This is a purposefully planned gathering in one of Richmond's six major business districts. With more than 22,000 daytime residents, Innsbrook represents an exciting opportunity. Currently, this small group, which we are using as a prototype, meets monthly in a private room in a restaurant during lunch hour. Our goal is to establish similar groups in other business districts that will meet, strategize, and pray for their colleagues and the business environment in their offices. This current outreach at Innsbrook is new, but the idea of geographic gatherings is not. It represents a concept we pray will be able to grow and expand to the other five business districts in Richmond.

This idea of business district ministry came to me some four years ago. I believe it is from God and could very well play a significant role in enabling the church to impact the culture for the kingdom. The idea came quickly, thoroughly, boldly, and with incredible motivation and excitement. God seemed right in the midst of it.

We had been praying about finding a way to expand the presence and impact of small groups in the various business districts of Richmond. We believed even then that the church would have to place significant emphasis on the marketplace in the years to come if it was to continue to reach the lost and remain relevant.

We held a Pastors' Council meeting to cast the vision for this outreach to the pastors. At that time, there were eighteen on our Pastors' Council. Within a week of that meeting, twelve of those eighteen pastors were on board with the concept. They agreed to come together in an interdenominational way that validated one of our basic principles, which is to have a kingdom mindset. It looked as though this outreach was a go. Concurrently, we had some staff turnover, including our Small Group Coordinator moving to Texas. Therefore, we were unable to execute the program at the time, but it has never left my mind. We are now close to being in the position to do so, and we hope to go to school on that Innsbrook group and go beyond it in the near future. Allow me to explain the concept.

As stated above, the Richmond business community is separated into roughly six geographical areas. For years, statistics have shown that the culture is leaving the church. There are, no doubt, many reasons for this truth. Nonbelievers often see the church as hypocritical. They see some Christians saying one thing and doing another. Many, particularly millennials, see the church as divisive, as they do not understand the concept of denominationalism. That's one reason we believe that an outreach executed from an interdenominational perspective in the work world would have great value.

Each of the twelve churches agreed to have a volunteer marketplace ministry coordinator lead its efforts in this outreach. All twelve churches would survey their congregations and determine where their memberships reside Monday through Friday from eight to five. We would then look to those churches to help us seed groups within each of these six business districts. The churches would be asked to appeal to their members to commit to groups in districts where they work as an outreach opportunity for the kingdom. With recommendations from the marketplace ministry coordinator, we would then train these small group leaders. We also anticipated that larger business districts would have more than one group initially, the other districts following suit later.

Each group would meet on a weekly basis. There would be an opportunity for fellowship and, because they came from different churches and workplaces, an opportunity for participants to get to know one another over breakfast or lunch. At these meetings there would be a time of personal sharing when they could even confidentially share difficult issues within their workplaces. There would be a time of support and prayer for one another, and there might also be a short study on some issue that would be motivational and marketplace related. The group members would then go back to work refreshed, renewed, and committed to living the principles and truths of Christ, allowing them to be the filters of their thoughts and actions.

The plan was that there would be small group meetings of eight to twelve members coming together three weeks out of four weeks per month. On the fourth week of a month, all the groups in a specific district would come together. If there were ten groups downtown, all ten would meet together in a conveniently located place, such as a private cafeteria in one of their office buildings, a restaurant, or a hotel meeting room. They would have a time for fellowship and sharing, and perhaps some worship. Then they would hear one of the twelve pastors give a short, encouraging message relevant to work. Over a period of twelve months, each of the twelve pastors would have the opportunity to visit each of the six district meetings.

The Christians attending those meetings would be encouraged to live out their faith in the workplace, to pray for one another and their co-workers, and to make wise, ethical decisions. They would be living, day-to-day, several of the Twelve Truths by which we live. Four of these are: 1) Have a kingdom mindset. The body of Christ is bigger than any church, denomination, or movement, 2) Marketplace ministry by marketplace people is God's plan, 3) We want to go where the lost are, and 4) Methods will change but the message never does.

As a result of the positive examples we believe the members of these groups will set in their workplaces, we expect seekers to be attracted to these co-workers, and ultimately to the meetings. This will help facilitate growth in the small groups and therefore the large monthly group meetings. Moreover, during the course of a year, the nonchurched seekers who find their way to groups would ideally be exposed to twelve biblically based pastors, thereby introducing them to a dozen potential church homes. How exciting!

Over the last forty years, several members of our Pastors' Council have retired, and we are currently considering others for membership. Regardless of the makeup of our Pastors' Council, I believe this interdenominational business district ministry model has incredible potential for the kingdom in any city in the USA, as well as in the entire developed world.

Another new outreach that will be connected to an older, effective one has to do with our Second Half Ministry. As mentioned previously, this ministry has grown from twelve men to more than 175, and from one location to four. Three groups are in Richmond and another is sixty miles away in what Richmond natives often refer to as "The Rivah." In this case The Rivah means the Urbanna area. When they meet, following an opening time of prayer, sharing and teaching, the group breaks up into roughly three to five smaller groups. They meet twice a month and are all about caring for one another, growing together in their faith, and serving in their communities.

In a previous chapter, I mentioned that this movement was started by Gordon Prior, a man who had been our family dentist for years and was about to retire. Gordon wanted to use his retirement to do what God had for him in the next phase of this life. It was obvious Gordon had a passion for the Lord and for his friends, including those friends who did not know the Lord. When he asked my opinion as to whether the Lord might have something for him to do in his retirement, I asked, "Why wouldn't God use the gifts he had given him to further his kingdom during this season of his life?" So, out of that desire and passion, Needle's Eye's Second Half outreach began with Gordon Prior at the helm.

Over the years, I've had a number of opportunities to meet with and address this group. Through some of these men, as well as many others, it has become apparent to me that when we reach a certain age, depending on our past and how well we've handled our relationships, our lives have the potential to go into a downward spiral. This does not happen necessarily because we are afraid to die. Christians usually are not afraid of death. I perceive this downward spiral most often in those who have reached a point in later years when they acknowledge open wounds and broken relationships that have not been healed. The longer we go without resolving issues, the deeper the pain goes and the stronger the bitterness grows. The more we think about the hurt we have caused or how we have been hurt, the wider the relational divide becomes. The longer this goes unaddressed, the greater the likelihood bitterness has of taking over. Hebrews 12:15 says, "See to it that no one misses the grace of God and that no bitter root grows up to cause trouble and defile many" (NIV).

Bitterness in this passage is referred to in an agrarian way as a root. I'm not an expert on gardening or farming, but I do know that when I look at shrubbery, I realize there is as much below the ground as there is above. That analogy is that to which the author of Hebrews is referring. Bitterness is like a root, an unseen cancer, and if it is not addressed, it not only hurts the person to whom it is attached, but the text says it "defiles many." If relationships aren't made right, if healing does not occur, people die painful deaths and not just physical deaths. At this stage of life, those who have lived with broken relationships experience even more pain and remorse because, in their thinking, the open wounds cannot be closed. As the author of Hebrews states, the root of bitterness defiles many because when bitterness rises up inside an individual, the personality of that person changes, and can potentially negatively affect all who may come in contact with the one who lives with bitterness.

Obviously, this indicates a significant need for relational healing in the lives of many of our older generation. Needle's Eye plans to address this need because we believe reconciliation of relationships is critical, and it cannot take place until the person seeking it understands its process. The only way to correctly understand the process is to truly understand that relationships are more important than any other aspect of our lives, and that a commitment to reconciled relationships must begin with healing the brokenness in the relationship with the One who made us.

Therefore, we plan to launch an outreach in the form of a seminar / workshop, which at this time we are calling the "Regrets, Redemption, and Reconciliation Seminar." It will address the regrets many of us have, and the reconciliation we need. The workshop will encourage participants not to let the hurt continue, but rather to address the issues that need to be addressed with those from whom they have become estranged, allowing them to live a redeemed, reconciled life, and to die well.

As I consider this outreach, I go back to our discussion in chapter 3 concerning the Spiritual PGA. We all have a need for peace, we all have a need for relief from guilt (and to be forgiven, and to forgive). We also have a need for acceptance. This is certainly more than true of those with open wounds. They need peace. They have a lot of guilt, and they need acceptance from the people they have hurt, or who have hurt them.

Chasing after power, wealth, and prestige seemed to be attractive at the time. However, as the clock ticks seemingly faster and faster toward midnight, the realization grows that it very well may have all been meaningless. We pray that this soon-to-be-available seminar will lead many to peace with their Maker and in their relationships, freedom from guilt, and the forgiveness and acceptance they so desperately need from family and friends. May broken relationships be healed, may sorrow and sadness fade, and may the Lord Jesus be praised as his Spirit makes all things new.

CHAPTER TEN

In Conclusion

To say that God has been gracious and faithful to Needle's Eye over these past forty-plus years would be an incredible understatement. When I reflect on our early years and the years since, I am awed by his love and the amazing things he has done through Needle's Eye and its people in this community I love. It has been an unexpected and undeserved privilege to serve my Lord Jesus Christ in this way!

As I bring this book to conclusion, I would like for us to look at four particular considerations that impact our lives and today's cultural landscape: diversity, technology, networks, and worldview. I do not profess to be an expert in any of these, technology in particular. Thankfully, half of our team is made up of millennials, so, fortunately, we have a number who are. This is a good thing, because in large measure our future will depend upon how we handle technology as well as diversity and networks. To that end, I want to say a few things about all three, and finish with a believer's perspective on the lens through which we see life, our worldview.

Diversity

Needle's Eye has always been concerned about, and committed to, diversity. For example, the first female member of our Board of Directors began her tenure in the early 1980s. Our first female Board Chair took the helm of the board in 1992. This happened naturally, without much, if any, thought or discussion about gender.

There also were inordinate opportunities with which to deal. Having grown up in Richmond, I knew an historic divide existed in the business community. In 1968, a group of African-American business owners began The Metropolitan Business League (MBL) because of their inability to join the Richmond Chamber of Commerce. In the 1980s, I was introduced to the Honorable James E. Sheffield, the first African-American Circuit Court Judge in Virginia since Reconstruction. Jim became a good friend and a member of our Advisory Board. On one occasion I shared with him my desire to reach the African-American business community because I felt God had not called us to minister merely to one segment of the Richmond marketplace. Rather, he wanted us to reach all of it.

Jim promptly introduced me to the President and CEO of the MBL at that time, Lynda Sharp Anderson. Lynda and I began a friendship that continues today. She has been a speaker for us and also serves on our Advisory Board. Because of my relationship with Lynda, I have been able to meet several leaders of The Metropolitan Business League.

These types of relationships are rich, but as is the case with all relationships, they require time and nurturing. Sometimes, the press of day-to-day responsibilities can overshadow things that are, and ought to be, considered more important. I must confess that has certainly happened to me on occasion regarding this issue.

In an earlier chapter, I wrote that prayer is one of God's truths by which we have operated for more than forty years. As such, Needle's Eye played a significant role in fostering a prayer movement in the eighties and early nineties. Many of the church leaders and individuals who played important roles in that effort were people of color, and a number of the relationships made at that time continue today. The Movement, as we knew it then, sponsored a citywide Concert of Prayer at the Arthur Ashe Center in

Richmond in which more than sixty churches participated. Subsequently, there were follow-up interdenominational pastors' prayer meetings over the next four years, and the regular second Saturday of the month Concert of Prayer continued until September 2000.

Twenty-plus years ago, workplace diversity in Richmond primarily meant the inclusion of African-Americans and women. This was reflected in Needle's Eye's makeup. However, in recent years things have changed significantly. The Metropolitan Richmond Region is comprised of just fewer than 1.3 million people. Of that number, about 95,000 residents are either Asian (3.6 percent) or Latino (3.9 percent). This represents a noteworthy amount of our population (7.5 percent), and, therefore, our workforce.[1]

Going forward, we need to make more of an effort to reach those in our target audience from these ethnic groups. We also must focus more of our board recruiting effort in this direction by utilizing our Leadership Development Initiative (LDI, see the addendum).

I share this information to provide historical context relative to where we are today. As our society becomes more diverse, and as believers understand the biblical view of diversity, we remember that "there is neither Jew nor Greek, slave nor free, male nor female, for you are all one in Christ Jesus" (Gal 3:28 NIV). This has been the case since the first century, and in today's culture it seems to have become even more critical, desirable, and important.

To address this issue directly and aggressively, but also to remain true to our Board Selection Criteria, Needle's Eye formed a committee two years ago that we call our Leadership Development Initiative. It is chaired by one of our board members and is tasked with cultivating and combing the Richmond marketplace for well-qualified prospective members for the Needle's Eye Board. The goal is to provide a steady stream of candidates to be presented to the board for consideration. These candidates are to represent all groups to be found in the area we serve, candidates who meet all our criteria.

1. Data from the Greater Richmond Partnership, https://www.grpva.com/data-reports/regional-demographics/.

When we identify someone in whom we may be interested, the candidate is vetted according to the individual's understanding of our mission and values statements, the desired criteria for board membership, and our statement of faith (The National Association of Evangelicals). Viable candidates are cultivated by board members who do so by acquainting them with the different ministry opportunities of Needle's Eye. The candidates also are introduced to the other board members who aid in the cultivation process by striving to build relationships with them. At the appropriate time, a prospect's name will be added to a somewhat vetted list of candidates—a list that is continually circulated among the Board of Directors.

We believe it is critical for board members to satisfy the requirements of each item listed on the Desired Criteria for Board Members sheet (see Addendum). Perhaps the most difficult criterion is number four—"Someone who has been touched by the Lord through the Ministry of Needle's Eye." Although this is less likely to have happened than the other three, in our view, this is the most critical. It fosters buy-in, ownership, and understanding, along with a solid commitment to the mission of Needle's Eye. It's nonnegotiable, and therefore is one of the main reasons LDI is so important.

Technology

With respect to technology, the best and most concise statement I have heard concerning its importance in today's culture was made by Ken Banks, a former board member of Needle's Eye and founder of IPC Technologies, a Richmond-based company that has a national presence through its connection with Shoretel. When asked about the importance of technology and how it should undergird Needle's Eye, Ken said, "The Internet is the largest information store in the world. With a cell phone, I can retrieve anything, anywhere. Safari is the most important point on the Home Page."

Volumes of information are available anywhere, any time. Technology provides the means to get a message out, whatever the message may be—to one's constituents, to interested nonaffiliates, to the masses, or perhaps to family, friends, and co-workers. Today there are no boundaries that limit our access to information, the means of disseminating information, or the applications that can be created to make information immediate, compelling, and relevant to people with particular interests and needs.

The first time Henrico County police patrolman Doug Middleton saw a computer back in 1972, he thought to himself, "This would be incredible in a patrol car." Today, Colonel Douglas Middleton, retired Chief of Police of the fourth largest county in Virginia, ups the ante when speaking about technology: "Embrace it, or you will lose your place."

As with the need for diversity, Needle's Eye has always been concerned about technology. We embrace it with all its capabilities and frustrations. As a ministry that covers the age gambit from millennial to boomer and beyond, we use everything from mass monthly e-news emails, to targeted social media boosts. We are on Facebook, LinkedIn, and all other relevant social media outlets. For years we have held semi-annual training meetings for our approximately sixty small group leaders. We now periodically make five- to ten-minute training videos.

Currently, the content we are managing and disseminating through technology encompasses several categories. Our primary outreaches (i.e., speaker events) and growth opportunities (i.e., a seminar on sharing your faith, etc.), are regularly featured in our monthly e-newsletter. Once that is distributed to some 2500 subscribers, we then put it into a blog post. Additionally, we will on occasion feature an article on a local businessperson addressing a workplace or community issue. As previously mentioned, we send short training videos to small group leaders and also promotional videos of upcoming speakers and events to our email list. These are subsequently posted for future use.

Recently, we considered live streaming our Speaker Series. Held during the lunch hour, these events address relevant workplace problems and issues. We thought this might benefit those unable to break away and attend. Because the series is just being reactivated, we decided against doing so at this time as we did not want to negatively affect attendance. However, once the series has been underway a while, and has a good, consistent base of attendees, live streaming will likely become a staple.

Additional ministry technology applications are endless. Given our emphasis on whole life discipleship, I believe weekly devotional podcasts geared to workplace issues would be a viable possibility. Interactive online training for our entire constituency on topics such as living one's faith in the workplace and personal evangelism could reach more people and complement the seminars we provide in person.

However, we do not want online forums to take the place of personal connections. As Needle's Eye Board member Shawn Boyer, founder of Snagajob and the new life planning app, goHappy, once stated to me, "These beginning opportunities can be starters or supplements to help people within Needle's Eye to connect." They could also enhance current programs or a person's involvement due to the ease of access. Shawn went on to say, "Bite-size chunks of technology, at the right time, at the right place, with the right vehicle, could have a profound impact on a large or specific group of people."

Here is one possible example. Throughout the last half of 2016 and the majority of 2017, the board of Needle's Eye walked through stage four breast cancer with one of our board members. Through it all, she was a shining light of God's love and trust in him. She even spoke for us at a citywide meeting on one of UVA Basketball Coach Tony Bennett's, "Five Pillars for Success." Thankfulness was her topic! Although her complete message is up on our website, a short video of her deep trust in God and her valiant fight would most certainly have been more than moving to many.

The Lord has blessed us with representation from all corners of the marketplace. Within our constituency are a number of well-known and well-respected people. Another possible use of technology would be to make videos of these civic and business leaders addressing current and difficult issues. These would likely be informative and enlightening to many, especially if released when particular topics are in the news and top of mind.

Finally, technology can create the means for a perfect connection between people with shared interests and passions. This would likely be attractive to those who have been unable to connect for whatever reason, such as certain affinity groups. An extension of this thought could be a hybrid ministry model. Basically, it would combine individual technology access with a live corporate meeting that would complete the series. For example, let's say Needle's Eye was holding an October citywide breakfast to unpack the attributes that apply to business people contained in the book of Philippians. Initially, we would promote the fall event through a daily/weekly blog of some 150 to 200 words. All those who followed the blog (and perhaps some others) would be encouraged to come together for the event in the fourth week. Prior to the breakfast, questions to be addressed at the meeting would be distributed to all the potential participants.

The possibilities are endless when it comes to the utilization of technology. Needle's Eye has been committed to it for years and will remain so. As Ken Banks once said to me in a lunch meeting, "People have access to unlimited information for validation." As Christians, we are members of God's family—children of the King. Therefore, we should not need to be validated. Rather, we need to use the tools of technology to enhance the growth of the kingdom both in its depth and in its numbers.

Networking

Networks and networking were important in the business world long before I joined the Jaycees (Junior Chamber of Commerce) as a young businessman in the early 1970s. With the increase of technology transfer capabilities, the opportunities to connect with and influence others are close to incomprehensible. However, technology is not the only means of networking. Personal relationships remain the preferred option. As mentioned earlier, Needle's Eye is currently involved with six other networks of marketplace millennials in the Metropolitan Richmond Region. We have belonged to the Richmond Chamber of Commerce for years and the Chamber's younger membership is one of the seven in the network. Only Needle's Eye and one other entity are faith-based, but we have taken the initiative of drawing the leaders of each of these groups together for a meet-and-greet planning lunch. The purpose is to grow relationships and thereby have an impact on the members of each group as well as the community at large. Obviously, technology will play a major role in the sharing of information and the drawing together of the networks or groups for common purposes. We are particularly excited about what this network of networks could mean for the kingdom and, consequently, for the community as a whole.

For years we have believed in and used networks as vehicles of ministry communications and delivery. Our Pastors' Council, which is comprised of pastors from about eighteen churches representing ten different denominations, has been in operation for over twenty-five years. There also are another thirty or so churches supportive of Needle's Eye that we ask to help in communicating our various outreach opportunities.

Additionally, we have had an Advisory Board since 1990. This was originally established to create a group of believers working within all sectors of the marketplace. They would, in turn, be able to offer Needle's Eye advice on how best to reach each member's individual sector. We purposely recruited members from areas of the marketplace including finance, law, manufacturing, government, medicine, education, small business ownership, marketing, and large corporations. The Advisory Board normally meets twice a year and provides input and direction as well as mutual encouragement.

As mentioned earlier, we will be bringing back Peer Group luncheons this year. These are meetings of particular professional affinity groups: lawyers, business owners, dentists, real estate agents, and the like. They are sponsored and hosted by three or four Christians within the particular group. Their purpose is to introduce colleagues to Needle's Eye and hopefully at some point to the Lord. The opportunities for ministry through social media within the Advisory Board, as well as within select peer groups, are exciting and intriguing. Devotional podcasts, business issue-driven videos, and opportunities for cross-pollination of groups only begin to touch the surface of unlimited possibilities.

Networks and networking can produce positive results for a community when done purposefully. Over the years, we have seen this principle at work in a number of initiatives, including the establishment of the CrossOver Healthcare Ministry and the prayer movement that led to the citywide Concert of Prayer in which we participated in 1993. Going forward, it will definitively take a collaborative effort to implement the vision of business-district small group ministries, with groups initially seeded by members from a number of churches representing multiple denominations. As I look into the future and contemplate our vision for Richmond, I see another collaborative effort on the horizon. Richmond has a number of committed and effective parachurch ministries carrying out the visions that God has laid on their hearts. Remember, a parachurch is not a church, but rather a ministry that reaches a specific target audience, filling a certain void that the church is currently not filling. Recently, I believe the Lord has laid on my heart the opportunity to be part of those parachurch ministries embracing a similar vision for the community, and like-minded theology, to see where he might take the group. This could be really exciting, even amazing!

Over the years, we have worked at being seen as interdenominational in order to project and model a kingdom mindset. We believe that purposefully using networks within the Christian community and collaborating for kingdom purposes will enable the soil of our city and its surrounding jurisdictions to be seeded with the love of Christ and the truth of the gospel. We will continue to do so as we move into the future.

A Biblical Worldview and Our Vision

The day I came to Christ, my life and the way I viewed life began to change. For the first time I began to understand the concept of "a peace that passes all understanding" (Phil 4:6) even in the midst of difficulty. My deep-seated guilt was gone, and I had been forgiven (1 John 1:8–9). I began to realize that God accepted me, not because of my performance, but because of his love for me (Rom 5:8). This realization, these significant truths, change the way one lives, the way one views life and, therefore, the world. No longer were power, wealth, and prestige my motivators and goals. The indwelling Spirit of Christ was making me "a new creation; the old has gone, the new has come" (2 Cor 5:17)! Everything was changing, including the way I viewed history, my life in the now, and what was really important about the future. My values became different. Relationships had the potential for healing. There would now be at least one in every two-person relationship who realized his sinfulness and was willing (most of the time) to be the first to admit wrong and ask for forgiveness. The desire to live for oneself, to be one's own god, began to dissipate as the one true God showed me his presence, power, faithfulness, and love. By his grace my life had been forever changed, so how could I ever again view the world, with its false gods and love of self, the same? My way of life and my worldview became different. Tim Keller, in his book about faith and work, *Every Good Endeavor,* says, "But a worldview is not merely a set of philosophical bullet points. It is essentially a master narrative, a fundamental story about a) what human life in the world should be like, b) what has knocked it off balance, and c) what can be done to make it right."[2]

For me, Genesis 1–2 and Revelation 21–22 depict what the world and its inhabitants should and will be like. Genesis 3 is the foundational text for what caused everything to get out of balance. Matthew 27–28 depict what has been accomplished in order to make it right. Obviously, my worldview and that of Needle's Eye

---

2. Tim Keller with Katherine Leary Alsdorf, *Every Good Endeavor* (New York: Penguin, 2012), 155–56.

is a biblical one. Scripture is self-authenticating. Second Timothy 3:16–17 says, "All Scripture is God-breathed . . ." Therefore, I/we believe that all humankind has sinned and therefore is separated from God (Rom 3:23), that God's son Jesus died for our sins (John 3:16), and those who believe in him are new and ever-changing believers called to be his ambassadors (2 Cor 5:17–21). Those who have experienced the new life in Christ are given a great commandment: "Love the Lord your God with all your heart and with all your soul and with all your mind . . . and love your neighbor as yourself" (Matt 22:37, 39). Can you imagine what our country and our cities, even the world, would look like if the church not only knew, but actively lived these truths?!

In February 2018, after six months of prayer and discussion, the Board of Directors of Needle's Eye approved our first vision statement. We have had a mission statement that has remained virtually the same ever since the beginning of our ministry. About twenty years ago, we added a values statement (see Addendum). Vision statements are the result of what could or should occur by living out one's mission. In one of our visionary sessions, a board member said that a vision statement is "the milk and honey of the mission." Needle's Eye's vision statement is:

> "To see Metro Richmond prosper and rejoice[1] through the transformed lives[2] of men and women passionately pursuing Jesus Christ[3] in their workplaces."[4]

When reproduced in its initial and intended form, the numerals indicated above do not exist. I have added them here in order to impart understanding and depth to a vision statement that we pray will ultimately come to fruition.

1. "Prosper and rejoice" comes from Proverbs 11:10, which states, "When the righteous prosper, the city rejoices." The word "righteous" in this context refers not to those who try to keep the law and are seen as holier than thou. Rather, it refers to those who desire to follow God, knowing their need for him. Commentators also say that in this context the word "prosper" refers to financial prosperity. It makes sense that

the population of a city or metropolitan area would rejoice if those following hard after God realize that what is theirs is actually his, and therefore the needs of people become more important to them than their own portfolios.

2. How could this happen in our self-absorbed society? Those who are righteous are so because their lives have been changed by the spirit of the Risen Christ. They are new creations and his ambassadors (2 Cor 5:17–21). They desire to follow Jesus closely by obeying all that he has commanded (Matt 28:19–20). This process of discipleship is enabled, and will continue to be, as they present their bodies as living sacrifices and are transformed by the renewing of their minds (Rom 12:1–2).

3. This results in a mindset in which they want to be crucified with Christ, knowing that they no longer live for themselves, but for him, because he loved them so much that he died for them (Gal 2:20). Consequently, Christ now lives in them and they are not ashamed of the gospel (Rom 1:16). They passionately share it in word and deed, giving themselves up for their neighbors.

4. When believers purposefully pursue Jesus in their workplaces, workplaces change. Jesus Christ is the only one who can change lives, and changed lives change culture. Living Christ's ethics and love on the job makes the teachings of God our Savior attractive (Titus 2:9–10). Marketplace people touch many lives from co-workers to clients to providers. Marketplace leaders have networks of influence through which countless numbers potentially can be touched and impacted by the gospel . . . and changed lives cause the city to rejoice!

Lord Jesus, may the current outreaches of Needle's Eye, as well as ones to come, be tools in your hands to help this vision become a reality, by your grace, and for your glory.

Amen!

Addendum

Calling: A Variety of Experiences

Taken from The Word in Life Study Bible
Thomas Nelson Publishers, 1996; Page 1379

Person	Occupation at the Time of God's Calling	Result of God's Call
Abraham	Unknown	Left his homeland and relocated to Canaan by way of Haran. (Gen. 11:31–12:4; Acts 7:2–5)
Isaac	Wealthy owner of livestock	Remained in the land of Canaan, where he carried on his father's faith and work. (Gen. 26:2–6)
Jacob	Wealthy owner of livestock	Lived with the hope that the God of his father and grandfather would bring him back in peace to the land of Canaan. (Gen. 28:12–29:1; 33:18-20)
Moses	Adopted son of the royal family of Egypt; sheepherder in Midian	Became the liberator and leader of the Israelites. (Ex. 3:1–12; 5:1)
Nehemiah	Cupbearer to the Persian king Artaxerxes I (see Neh. 1:11)	Negotiated with the king to lead a group of Jews back to Jerusalem to rebuild the city, particularly its walls. (Neh. 1:1–2:10)
Esther	Wife of King Ahasuerus of Persia	Intervened to save the lives of her people, the Jews, from a genocidal plot. (Est. 4:1–6:10)

Ezekiel	Priest	Became a prophet, speaking God's message to the Jewish exiles in Babylon. (Ezek. 2:1–5)
Daniel	A youth deported to Babylon	Became an advisory to kings, and a prophet. (Dan. 1:19; 7:1)
Jonah	Unknown	After initially running from the Lord, went to Nineveh and warned of God's judgement, resulting in citywide repentance. (Jon. 1:1–3; 3:1–10)
Rich Young Ruler	Member of Israel's upper class	Turned away from the Lord because he could not bring himself to part with his possessions. (Matt. 19:16–22)
Barnabas	Unknown	Served as a friend and mentor to young believers, including Saul. (Acts 9:26–27; 11:25–26) and John Mark (15:36–39)
Saul	Tentmaker: Pharisee leading anti-Christ activities	Became God's principal spokesman during the latter part of the first century A.D. (Acts 9:15)
Believers in General	Varied	Brought to salvation through faith in Christ; a transformed lifestyle. (Rom. 1:6–7; 8:28–30; 12:1–2)

Most of our biblical heroes (some of whom are listed above), those whose stories we tell our children and grandchildren at bedtime, were neither prophets, priests, pastors, nor missionaries. They were regular people who loved God and wanted to serve him in and through their daily lives.

Theology of "Calling"

Greek form: Κλητός (klétos)

Occurs four times in Romans, ten times in the New Testament.

As an office or function—Romans 1:1; 1 Corinthians 1:1 = "called to be an apostle."

Called/invited

- Romans 1:6—". . . called to belong to Jesus Christ."

- Romans 1:7—". . . called to be saints."

- Matthew 22:14—"for many are invited (called, ESV), but few are chosen."

- 1 Corinthians 1:2—". . . those sanctified in Christ Jesus and called to be holy."

- Romans 8:28—". . . called according to his purpose."

- 1 Corinthians 1:24—"but to those whom God has called, both Jews and Greeks . . ."

- Jude 1—". . . to those who have been called, who are loved by God the Father and kept by Jesus Christ."

- Revelation 17:14—". . . with him will be his called, chosen and faithful followers."

As mentioned in chapter 4, *klétos* is a primary word for "call" in the New Testament. It occurs ten times but only twice in the role of a function ["Paul, called to be an apostle . . ."]. The other eight times, it is used in the context of relationship ("called to belong to Jesus Christ," "Called according to his purposes," "With him will be his called, chosen, and faithful followers."). Therefore, 80 percent of the times that *klétos* occurs in the New Testament, it occurs relative to being called to Christ. See chapter 4 for the implications of this truth.

Twelve Truths Over 40 Years:

God's Grid for Needle's Eye Ministries

- Prayer . . . the foundation of all we do.
  Ps 32:6–8; Php 4:6–7; Jas 1:5

- Trust God to meet all our needs.
  Prv 3:5–6; Php 4

- Obedience is critical . . . but it doesn't always equate with comfort.
  Gen 22:1–19; Acts 5:27–42

- Listen to the Spirit.
  John 16:13; 1 Cor 2:10–13

- Unanimity in board decision-making.
  John 17:20–23; Rom 12:2; Php 2:1–2

- Have a kingdom mindset. The body of Christ is bigger than any church, denomination, or movement.
  Rom 15:5–6; Eph 4:4–6

- God cares about the community in which we live—and so should we.
  Prv 11:10; Jer 29:7; Mat 25:31–46

- God's ways are often different than man's ways.
  Prv 16:9; Isa 55:8–11

- Marketplace ministry by marketplace people is God's plan.
  Ex 31:1-6; Acts 1:4-9;
  Col 3:22—4:1; Tit 2:9–10

- Meet the felt needs of your target audience, in order to meet the real need.
  Luke 8:38–39; 1 Cor 9:19–22, 10:31—11:1; Acts 2:42–47

- We want to go where the lost are!

  Luke 19:1–10; John 4:34–41

- Methods will change, the message never does!

  Acts 4:11–12; Heb 13:8; 1 Cor 9:22

**Reproduced with permission from The London Institute
for Contemporary Christianity**

As referenced in chapter 9, this is a wonderful tool to enable us to remember, pray about, and live out the principles of whole life discipleship. Mark Greene and the London Institute for Contemporary Christianity, among others, are doing much to keep this somewhat forgotten cultural and biblical concept squarely in front of us. This is so important as we live in a time of both great spiritual need as well as apathy and antagonism toward the gospel.

ADDENDUM

Desired Criteria for Needle's Eye Board Membership

- A committed believer who is a part of the business and professional community, and one who sees the need for this type of ministry
- A leader in their local church
- Currently, and hopefully for some time, actively involved in the ministry of Needle's Eye
- Someone who has been touched by the Lord through the ministry of Needle's Eye

Two sets of considerations need to be balanced in selecting board members. The reelection of persons who have previously served provides the important elements of continuity and familiarity with the work of the ministry. At the same time, in order to maintain a flow of new ideas, expand our base of ministry, and generally seek to provide new blood for Needle's Eye, it is vital to bring in first-time members. It has been suggested that it is prudent to select at least as many new directors as directors who have served before.

Leadership Development Initiative
Policies and Procedures

The Leadership Development Initiative ("LDI") is tasked with:

1. Cultivating the Richmond Marketplace for well-qualified prospective members of NEM's Board of Directors;

2. Providing a steady stream of qualified board candidates, representing all aspects and groups in Richmond's marketplace, to the ministry for consideration;

3. Tracking and evaluating the board's progress towards its responsibility to cultivate and provide the ministry with qualified board candidates.

The starting points for qualification for board membership will include . . .

- Acceptance, understanding, and excitement about our mission statement;

- Meeting the existing points on the "Desired Criteria for NEM Board Membership" sheet;

- Agreement with all points of our Statement of Faith.

When there are disagreements on issues relating to the infallibility of Scripture, they will be resolved through the lens of an evangelical theological perspective on the interpretation of said Scripture.

Procedurally, as the marketplace is cultivated, the first steps of the group's activities will be to encourage prospects to attend, and become involved in, NEM's one-time and ongoing ministry opportunities. Then, introducing prospects to other board members will be expected, as this will enhance the depth of relationships. The cultivation process is expected to take time; it is not a sprint.

This emphasis will become operative when the initiative is set and approved. The initiative is to be comprised of current and former board members. The LDI will be responsible to the Board of Directors of NEM and its Executive Committee. The Board of Directors is ultimately responsible for the development, recruiting, and assimilation of its members.

Current Mission Statement

Connecting marketplace men and women to life-changing faith in Jesus—encouraging them to impact their workplaces and our community with his values, ethics, and love.

Values Statement

Believing that a personal relationship with Jesus is the most important thing marketplace men and women can have, we:

1. Present the message of salvation though God's saving grace and love, especially by encouraging them to share their personal faith stories with others;

2. Encourage them to live out their faith in Jesus in every aspect of their lives, especially in their workplaces;

3. Provide Christ-centered biblical teaching, fellowship, and training to prepare them to impact their homes, workplaces, and communities spiritually, ethically, and morally; and

4. Promote the concept of marketplace ministry in partnership with local churches.

Vision Statement

To see Metro Richmond prosper and rejoice through the transformed lives of men and women passionately pursuing Jesus Christ in their workplaces.

Needle's Eye Ministries Is a Member of the National Association of Evangelicals. Their/Our Statement of Faith Is:

1. We believe the Bible to be the inspired, the only infallible, authoritative Word of God.

2. We believe that there is one God, eternally existent in three persons: Father, Son and Holy Spirit.

3. We believe in the deity of our Lord Jesus Christ, in His virgin birth, in His sinless life, in His miracles, in His vicarious and atoning death through His shed blood, in His bodily resurrection, in His ascension to the right hand of the Father, and in His personal return in power and glory.

4. We believe that for the salvation of lost and sinful people, regeneration by the Holy Spirit is absolutely essential.

5. We believe in the present ministry of the Holy Spirit by whose indwelling the Christian is enabled to live a godly life.

6. We believe in the resurrection of both the saved and the lost; they that are saved unto the resurrection of life and they that are lost unto the resurrection of damnation.

7. We believe in the spiritual unity of believers in our Lord Jesus Christ.